T0149527

THE *Practice* OF HIS RIGHTEOUSNESS

*The Essential Truths for Living
a Christian Life*

LEONEL DIEUJUSTE

iUniverse books may be ordered through booksellers or by contacting:

iUniverse
1663 Liberty Drive
Bloomington, IN 47403
www.iuniverse.com
1-800-Authors (1-800-288-4677)

Because of the dynamic nature of the Internet, any web addresses or links contained in this book may have changed since publication and may no longer be valid. The views expressed in this work are solely those of the author and do not necessarily reflect the views of the publisher, and the publisher hereby disclaims any responsibility for them.

Any people depicted in stock imagery provided by Thinkstock are models, and such images are being used for illustrative purposes only. Certain stock imagery © Thinkstock.

ISBN: 978-1-5320-3660-6 (sc)
ISBN: 978-1-5320-3662-0 (hc)
ISBN: 978-1-5320-3661-3 (e)

Print information available on the last page.

Library of Congress Control Number: 2017919605

iUniverse rev. date: 02/07/2018

Contents

Author's Word to the Reader

If you can endure the part that you may dislike, you will have the chance to greatly benefit from the many other parts that you do like. That is true in life and, also for this book.

♦ Introduction

Be Where You Are Needed— Focus on Destiny

Everyone needs a community made of other individuals in order to evolve and share the best of their abilities. Whether a community of friends and family, a group based on ethnicity, a business organization, a political association, or a spiritual assembly, whatever the basis of the gathering is, a change takes place in every one of the individuals gathered together. Some will experience more change than others due to personal drive and motivation, but a change will occur in the lives of all parties involved in a community.

A handful of institutions are fundamental to humankind for personal development. We have the educational institutions for personal intellectual growth. Professional institutions are responsible for the development of talents and personal gifts. And we have the cult. Of all institutions, the church, which is part of the cult, is the only one with the mandate from God to make a real difference in the world.

Everyone who ever made a great difference in the world has followed a discipline or adopted a spiritual guideline. Nothing happens unless you are connected to a higher knowledge or power.

Knowledge, in general, comes with a cost known as responsibility. For someone to act responsibly, good judgment always comes into play and many virtues that take time to develop. The result of good judgment and virtues is character. A person's character is his or her personal guide to a successful life. You may own the entire world, and the universe as surplus, but without good character, you are a danger to yourself. Many people place great value in building wealth in the form of academics and finance, but few consider an investment in the building of their characters. The character of those in a community determines the quality of life in that community. Therefore, the same way that we need the community to evolve, the community first needs us as members to evolve.

One needs to consider being part of the most affluent and influential group that will make a real difference in the world today. You may already be part of a social club. You may even be part of a local church. But you must know that no business association can promise a truly successful life. No government has the power to change the conditions of the human soul and mind for the better. No local church, unless operating under the dictate of the Holy Spirit in the Word of God, can make a positive difference in the world. Only the church that is both the individual and a community of saints can change a person's perspective and then help change the individual's attitude and behavior. No other institution holds that power.

If you already belong to the church, you need to know your standing and true purpose to be able to use your divine power. Knowledge is power only when possessed. What you don't know can, in fact, kill you.

The Christian Bible contains the oldest knowledge and discipline. Many, if not all, sources of knowledge have taken from that ancient book to make their own. The Bible goes all the way back to creation and recorded the first fallout of humankind with God.

Many books have been published to educate people about the Christian faith. Highly educated writers—people with master's degrees and doctorate—have clearly explained the phenomenon of being a follower of Christ. No more effort is truly needed there.

On the other hand, the divorce rate is high among members of the Christian church worldwide. We have so-called Christians living the same lifestyle and with the same principles as nonbelievers. We have a generation of young people with no spiritual values in part because an old generation left no good examples for the new one to follow. With the great lack of love in the world, we need true disciples of Christ. All efforts are needed there. Yours too.

This book is about making a difference in the lives of others by first making a difference in ourselves and in our character. It centers around good practice of the virtues taught in the Word of God to help us live better with each other in the spirit of forgiveness and love toward our neighbors. It is not enough simply to have

Topical biblical references—these are not the actual Bible verses. Check your favorite Bible edition for the exact translations.

To be approved by God: Those who commend themselves are not the ones who are necessarily approved. Rather, those who God commend are approved (cf. 2 Corinthians 10:17–18).

Higher competence: No one is found sufficient in himself or herself to do the great work of God. One is sufficient in God by the knowledge He has communicated to that person to enable him or her to do His great work (cf. 2 Corinthians 3:4–5).

Unfamiliar wisdom: The wisdom that those who are called by God have is not one that is found among the great rulers of our society but, rather, among the simple. That wisdom is a mystery to those who are considered important people of our world- (cf. 1 Corinthians 2:6–15).

Jesus and His conflict with the church: Jesus was not accepted by the traditional church of his time. They wanted Him dead (cf. 2 Corinthians 3:4–5).

Purposely chosen among fools: Throughout the Bible, those who God called were not among the great personalities of their societies. They were considered the lowest. Certainly, they have become greatly known. However, God and their callings made them great (cf. 1 Corinthians 1:26–29).

Matters of Divine Spirit: Those who God has called have also received the spirit of God, so they may understand the things of God. One cannot understand anything that comes from God without first receiving His spirit (cf. 1 Corinthians 2:11, 12, 13).

The unexpected career change by God: And God has taken some out from other areas and fields of work and placed them to work for Him as his prophets or disciples. Those who had no intention of becoming prophets were chosen by God to represent Him before others (cf. Amos 7:12–17).

business with each other and focus on our personal interests. We also need to look for what benefits others without any self-interest. This is not easy to achieve, and everyone will occasionally have a falling out with someone at work or at home. But if we know what the objective is and the most important things to focus on in life, we will make the effort necessary to achieve that objective. This book helps you focus on the objective of having the required relation with people and to achieve the peace and success we desire in our personal lives. It will also help you either to discover or penetrate deeper into your spirituality, which has a great importance to your happiness and success.

For the aspiring disciple, this book is about living for God and following the example of Jesus. It is the Christian faith in practice. It is Christianity in common terms for those who are unfamiliar with the subject. It is written for those who have so much knowledge that they have forgotten the basics. And it is also written for those, due to lack of practice, have chosen to ignore what once made a great difference in their lives. This book is not a good read. Rather, it is a good guide on how to put into action the living Word of God to make our lives not full but complete.

The Author's Credentials

If I were to have any qualifications based on human intellect, I would probably not have been able to write this book. Throughout the Bible, those who were not qualified based on human standards were called to do amazing things for God. He chose those individuals so there was no confusion whether the work they did was clearly seen to be accomplished by Him.

I cannot take any credit for writing this book aside from a personal willingness to obey God. I have been through diverse situations, and God has given me the wisdom to rise through it all. My education, although part of the divine plan, is not sufficient for the task of writing a spiritual book helping people gain knowledge in the things of God so they can live according to His Word and purpose. My line of study has involved mostly the artistic field. I have studied photography and fashion design. I attended Burdett College, a now-defunct business school in Boston. Although I was proud to complete my art degree at that school, I was more confident in being a Christian who will use my studies to make a stand for God and be an example of a new creature in Jesus.

My spirituality has always been my strongest attribute. However, I have always had conflict with the traditional church. I found great comfort knowing that Jesus was a carpenter with strong spiritual attributes who also had problems with the traditional church. Therefore, I feel biblically qualified as a firm believer in the awesome power of God and the teaching of Jesus to share my experience with you on how to succeed in life by following the wisdom of God. It is His wisdom that has given me the power to be not just successful but to choose to be a success. We have not been created to just be successful. God created us to carry out His glory on the earth. We were made to serve each other with our greatest potential, not as professional, but with our greatest character as a person. We were made to have not just professions but great personalities. We were made to use the many professions God called us to serve in.

It is the will of God that everyone be fruitful. Except for Jesus, no one, not even the characters of the Bible, is a perfect example of the righteousness God requires us to practice toward each other. No one ever fully practiced the justice that allows someone to constantly live in the awesome glory of God. However, such practice or discipline exists that guarantees humankind the ability to experience perfect peace and security. This high condition of living only comes with the knowledge and wisdom of God. The main purpose of this book is to point you toward the source of that knowledge. It also helps you take seriously the only lifestyle on earth guaranteed to enable people to live in perfect peace within themselves and then with others. I hope it fulfills that purpose for you.

SECTION 1

◆ Living the Glory of God

*God did not simply create man and woman just to
create something. He gave the man dominion and power
over the entire earth, as if the Creator of the universe
wanted someone to represent Him on this earth.*

Chapter Contents

Subject 1/Success Based on One's True Nature
Subject 2/Living the Glory of God
Subject 3/The Practice of Divine Faith

◆ Subject 1

Success Based on One's True Nature

1 The Bible dissects humankind as being three-dimensional in nature. We have the spirit, the inner being, or what we consider the real person inside. We have the soul, the set of emotions responsible for how we feel. And we have the physical body that represents us on the outside and how we become known to all around us.

Life is a journey that spans a two-dimensional world: the material world and the spiritual world. In the spiritual realm, everything is conceived as dreams, visions, or ideas. The soul makes it possible for humans to passionately live conceived dreams and ideas, and it enables us to express these dreams and ideas to all in living color. Our physical bodies help us to materialize our dreams and visions so that others can physically see and live these dreams as well.

Another great aspect to consider in humankind is our belief system, which we all know as faith. Everything we have experienced as great achievements

3

*Topical biblical references:*These are not the actual Bible verses. Check your favorite Bible version for the exact translation.

-1-

Real hope is that which is placed in God, and not the uncertainty of wealth (cf. 1 Timothy 6:17–19).

Riches here and beyond are treasures up in heaven where you are guaranteed to have them forever (cf. Matthew 6:19–24).

Do not chase money: Rather, chase righteousness and then money will come as a result (cf. 1 Timothy 6:6–16).

Envy not: The world's greatest troubles are caused by envy, wanting what we see others have (cf. James 4:1–4).

Honesty is priceless: The long-term consequences of being dishonest are way too severe (cf. James 5:1–6).

Seek first the kingdom of God: Better to seek God and his justice towards others. And all great things thus will follow (cf. Matthew 6:25–34).

was made possible by faith. We have come to know and enjoy great things simply because many of us at one time believed. It is impossible to achieve any conceivable achievement without first believing.

It is the will of God for everyone to prosper. True prosperity, however, comes with a great deal of understanding of what it really is. Otherwise, many find themselves always chasing something without knowing what they are looking for. And they will always be frustrated even though to many others, these individuals seem very successful.

To fully satisfy any animal, you must know what it eats. You will not fill your gasoline-powered vehicle with diesel and expect it to run. Certainly, you may have a full tank, but that car does not run with that type of fuel. In the same way, a pocket full of money will not necessarily make your soul happy. What may look like a success to others might make you miserable. All simply because you need to understand the true nature of humankind and what it takes to really satisfy your entire three-dimensional being. We must learn how not to satisfy one part of ourselves and leave the two other parts hungry.

There are many ways to fool yourselves with temporary happiness. True joy, however, will not be fulfilled by playing tricks. The last drop of a bottle of fine wine, for those who drink, will not give you contentment. Even the most beautiful wedding with the true love of your heart will only last a moment of joy. Real fulfillment come not with great achievements but with wisdom and great understanding. The knowledge of the biblical and scientific principle of sowing and reaping. The art of reciprocity; to do unto others as you would like others to do onto you. To love even those who mistreat you. To do good toward all. These things are not the products of happiness. We do not act good toward others after we reach our predetermined levels of success. Rather, they are the seeds that produce the success and joy we all look for. You will not become the nicest person after you graduate from school and become the best in your profession. Chances are, if you were a nasty and mean person before, you will remain so after. The only difference is after you are a success, you perhaps have a greater circle of people to be mean and nasty to. Money or success doesn't change a person. Rather, it amplifies the personality they already had.

True success embraces all the aspects of the life of the person who achieves it. Real success is meaningful and carries a purpose that benefits more than one person or small group. Those who are blessed are so they may be a blessing to others. Before one thinks about becoming a success, he or she must first be willing to submit to an area of service to others. Success will then bring real satisfaction. The individual must also try to find real joy and happiness away from that success. Real joy comes from contentment. To achieve that, one needs to understand divine faith. That is, one needs to have some ancient knowledge from the Bible, the Word of God. Without divine faith, it is impossible to be content because no amount of success or material possessions will produce contentment. Money solves a lot of problems, except those that are serious. For instance, money will not save your marriage, raise your dead child, or make your spouse be faithful. Money may provide the best education, but it will not give you common sense. If you didn't have wisdom before you became rich, money won't help you gain wisdom. You are more likely to gain a lot more wisdom by losing the money. Jesus, for example, asked a young rich man to lose the money and follow him. The apostle Paul asked those who were rich in his time almost the same thing. Money is not the key to what everyone is looking for. The Bible says to seek first the kingdom of God.

The following texts and questions open your eyes onto another dimension. Anyone with a little spiritual background will understand what this is all about. If you do not consider yourself a spiritual person, you will no longer be completely ignorant of this ancient world of divine faith, otherwise known as the Christian world.

◆ Subject 2
Living the Glory of God

What Is the Glory of God?

2 If you have doubts about the Bible and how it became, that's fine. For you to understand this, all you need is at least a little doubt about you coming from a monkey, which is how evolutionists explain the beginning of humankind. You also must accept the facts that there is far more knowledge than what you have come across, and that good and evil exist.

In the beginning, the Bible says God created the universe. Then He created all the animals. When it came to man, God said, "Let's make man in our image." This also tells you that the godhead has more than one person. The Bible explains that also. So man was created in the image of God. The same God who created the entire universe created man in His image. That could explain the creativity inherent in the nature of humans. We take that straight from God. Then came the woman, and she was taken straight

Topical biblical references: These are not the actual Bible verses. Check your favorite Bible version for the exact translation.

-2-

A real paradise—the garden of Eden—is where God placed Adam to work and evolve into the marvelous creature that God has wanted him to be for His glory (cf. Genesis 2:8–15).

One simple rule God has set for Adam to follow: The consequences for breaking that rule, however, result in spiritual death, which later becomes physical death (cf. Genesis 2:16–17).

Adam's wife, Eve, was tempted by the devil, who approached her in the form of a serpent. She was tricked into violating the only rule set by God to live in peace in paradise. And the show goes on from that point on (cf. Genesis 3).

7

-3-

Lucifer, otherwise known as the devil, is the highest of intelligence among angels. The most magnificent of beauty among them all. He is also called the accuser of the brethren, meaning that he's constantly pointing the finger at humankind before God to show Him how messed up we are. His main plan is to confuse us away from the truth and the will of God, so we may all be condemned with him in hell (cf. Isiah 14:12–15; 2Thessalonians 2:9-12; Job 1:1-10; Ezekiel 28:12-19; Jude 1:6

out of the man to be one with the him, not just a partner.

God did not simply create man and woman just to create something. He gave the man dominion and power over the entire earth, as if the Creator of the universe wanted someone to represent Him on this earth. God also let man name all the animals. He `also named the woman. Man and God ruled the earth. Man was living the glory of God.

Then, as the Bible explains, evil became known to man through an angel named Lucifer, who appeared in the form of a serpent. The serpent did not go to the man, whose name was Adam. Instead, the serpent approached the woman, Eve. Lucifer led the woman to believe that God was not honest with them and that the same God who created man and woman in His image really did not want them to be like Him. And Eve believed it. She went against God and convinced Adam to do the same. They disobeyed the one rule the Creator God has established for them. They were punished for going against God's original plan. They were evicted from the well-furnished garden where God placed them. They were now away from the presence of God and without His help. Humankind were no longer in the glory of God.

What Kind of Angel Is Lucifer, and Why Did He Do What He Did?

3 The Bible explains that Lucifer is a fallen powerful angel. He was honored greatly among the angels. He felt he had too much power to submit himself to God.

So he decided to set his throne above God's throne and rule over all God created. With all the power he had, it was dangerous to have that much pride. His pride has cost him his position in heaven. God cast him out, along with one third of the less-powerful angel under Lucifer's submission.

Lucifer hated the fact that his plan failed and that God was proven more powerful than he. He could not defeat God in heaven, and when his final judgment comes, he will be sentenced to hell for eternity. Since he could not defeat God Almighty, he vowed to ruin God's precious creation and turn humankind against the Creator. He knew how much God loves humankind and that they are the only creatures—besides God's only Son—created in His image. He also resented the fact that we have so much power. So he tricked man through his woman to rebel against God. That plan succeeded, and the relationship between God and humankind has been broken since.

What Became of the Relationship between God and Us?

4 After Adam and Eve sinned against God, they were separated from Him. They lost the presence of He who created them along with all the benefits that came with it. Humankind, created in the image of God, was never expected nor provisioned to live away from the presence of its Creator. All that is essential for our well-being is found in God Himself. Everything necessary to live well is packaged with

-4-

Humanity was condemned to sin after the fall of Adam. Human nature has become sinful in nature, and it has since been impossible for humankind to adhere to well doing. The law that is imposed on us cannot be kept for we have lost our innocence forever (cf. Romans 7:14–24; Judges 2:19; Nehemiah 1:7).

them being in a good relationship with God. After all, it is His Spirit that God placed in them. The carnal human, which is human in the flesh, was condemned to hard labor. But the human in spirit form, or the spirit person, experienced a much greater pain than the physical human. The spirit human was alienated.

A way for Adam and Eve to cope with being separated from God never seemed to be found. It wasn't until after four thousand years and many great disasters that God provided Himself, a way to reconnect the spirit human with Him.

Different methods were certainly introduced. The law of Moses and animal sacrifices came about. The last solution was for someone who never committed any sin to offer himself in sacrifice for the remission of sins of all humankind. Someone had to die a terrible death to reconcile humankind with God. Jesus volunteered, came, suffered, and died for us all. And now, in the name of Jesus, no more sacrifice is needed. We can all find ourselves one again with our Creator and regain all the benefits that include. No more being lost and estranged on the surface of the earth. At least there is no need to.

♦ Subject 3

The Practice of Divine Faith

Why Consider Being a Christian?

5 The word "Christian" means followers of Christ. Since Jesus is the one man who reconnected us to God, He was the only man able to show us the way to stay connected with the Creator. Jesus has become the mediator between humankind and God. He is not just a man. He is the only Son of God, the very first creation of the Almighty. The Bible says that in Him and for Him all things were created. He is the only one qualified to help us regain our rights to be the sons and daughters of God.

It is also in the name of Jesus that we can find and claim all we lost in the garden, where Adam and Eve sinned. Jesus came not only to die but also to show us how to live with the fact that we are still vulnerable to sins and the tricks of the devil.

We need to follow Jesus and all His instructions on how to avoid losing our place with God again.

Why accept Christ? Because in Him we have found redemption. He has made possible the forgiveness of our sins and reconnects us with God (cf. Ephesians 1:7; Colossians 1:14; Mark 10:45; Colossians 2:9–10).

-6-

The disciples were called Christians for the first time in the city of Antioch where Paul and Barnabas joined together and taught many new converts (cf. Act 11: 25–26).

Jesus, the only Son of God, firstborn or heir of His creations. God's only begotten Son in whom He placed all His power (cf. John 1:3; Colossians 1:16; Romans 8:29).

-7-

Making a practice of sin cannot be after accepting Jesus as savior. Certainly, human nature will cause everyone to sin. However, one should adopt a different standard of living once in Christ (cf. 1 John 3:4–10; 2 John 1:9).

Staying connected to Jesus is to live the Christian life. The born-again Christian must be attached to Jesus and His teaching to succeed (cf. John 15:5

Can Just Anyone Be Called a Christian?

6 Many claim to be Christians. But just like any other discipline that exists, there are certain formalities that enable a person to be taken seriously for what he or she claims to be. One is considered born again as soon as that person accepts Jesus as Lord and Savior. However, once anyone is prayed for and joins the family of Christ, there is a certain discipline to follow to fully benefit from the new life just entered. There are some truths that are essential to living a born-again Christian life, and a clear majority of people, although they might be considered in the circle of friends of the church, are not part of the family of Christ.

What Does It Mean to Be a Christian?

7 To be a Christian is the highest standard in the spiritual realm. The Christian is a totally free individual yet enslaved by the same set of rules that made him or her free. However, the new bondage that the born-again Christian has entered is nothing compared to the bondage the person is freed from. That is what makes Jesus the true Savior of humanity. Only Jesus can free someone from the bondage of the guilt of doing wrong, whatever that wrong may have been.

Not only are you freed from your old criminal status, you are given the opportunity to become part of the highest class in the society of humankind. And God, the sole Creator of the universe and the highest power of all the powers, has promised not to remember your crime or sin ever again. This, in Christian terms, is called "redemption." Christ redeemed us from the old bondage of lies and deceptions and placed us in a new bondage of truth and great promises. Being a Christian is a complete transformation from a shameful person to the most glorious character.

True Christianity Is a Complete Rebirth

8 What is the bondage of being a disciple of Jesus Christ? What are the demands that qualify an individual from the lost world to truly becoming an authentic Christian?

To answer these questions, we again point to the difference of being saved and becoming a born-again child of God. Anyone compelled by the spirit of God to be reinstated into His divine family only needs to confess publicly that Jesus is Lord and believe in his or her heart that God resurrected Jesus from the dead. You must have been indulged in and believe the story of Jesus. And you must once make a public confession that Jesus is Lord. That qualifies you to being saved from the lost world and reinstated into the family of God.

However, to be a true disciple of Christ and honestly carry the title of being a true Christian takes a process. One is saved instantly. However, one is

-8-

People of the highest standard. An elect individual, due to his personal interest in the affairs of God, and given a new vision and a new job to inspire others to enter the kingdom of God- *Cf. 1 Peter 2:9-12; Romans 8:30; Romans 3:23*

Slaves of righteousness is one who submits himself, against his nature, to live according to the new person desired by God. - *Cf. Romans 6:17-18; Romans 6:22; 1 Peter 2:16; Galatians 5:13*

_-9-_

From shame to glory- _The born-again Christian has changed from the status of being the enemy of God to now being son or daughter of God. A new status that give the person equal inheritance of God with Jesus-_ **Cf. Romans 8:10-17; Romans 8:17; Ephesians 2:19**

To be born again _is a process of becoming anew._ **-Cf. John 3:3; Romans 6:6; Colossians 3:10; Ezekiel 11:19; John 3:6-8; Titus 3:5-8**

To be set apart _from the old ways, and the world-_ **Cf. 1 Peter 2:9; John 17:15-18; John 15:19; Ephesians 4:22-24; Leviticus 18**

a Christian by a firm and honest conviction that the person has made to follow the instructions or commandments of God in a new life made possible by Jesus. To be a Christian is a complete rebirth. You know nothing on the same basis you had before, and you have come to practice all in an entirely new way. Christianity affects every aspect of the lives of those who choose to join this new society of saints. It is the world of the followers of Christ. It is the world of discipleship for the kingdom of God. It is your entire old world redefined.

Why We Do What We Do

9 The only difference between the world's ways of doing and the godly way of doing is in the definition of what they are doing and the purpose behind their actions. The circular world and the Christian world have their own distinctive definitions for all aspects of life that are important to how they function and live on this earth. The ways and reasons you do all things are derived from how you define the many aspects of life. People conceive certain definitions and adopt purposes before engaging in any action in their lives. Based on those definitions and purposes, the success or failure of those aspects of their lives is clearly determined. And unless a person's definition of something and the purpose for doing such are changed, the outcome or reality resulting from that action remains the same. For example, your definition of work and your purpose for working determine your level of success from work. The same is true for marriage or anything else you might consider in life. Your joy or burden, your success or failure all come from how you define and conceive things.

Thus, it is important that those aspiring to live as Christians set their lives apart and clearly discern the true definitions and purposes of their actions without any corruption from the circular world. Christian individuals are not to do or even consider the most basic thing as life the way the secular world does. We are not to function like the world since our purposes and definitions of all that matter are not the same.

In this book are a few factors in life that are very important to the functioning of the society of humankind and the Christian definitions and true purposes behind them. Changes made in these definitions to fit our purpose are what cause all the chaos we see in our world's society. For it written, "Do not add to what I command you and do not subtract from it, but keep the commands of the LORD your God that I give you." Deuteronomy 4:2 New International version (NIV). Few other scriptures in the Holy Bible warns us about the consequences of changing what God has established as standard. All humankind ought to practice standard correctness in all aspects of life, that which is considered the righteousness of God. The basic standard in every aspect of life has been predetermined by the Higher Power, who created all things. A godhead or divine being responsible for everything that exists. We are to adopt and practice these basic standards in our lives if we wish to experience the joy and success that come along with them. As it is written: "Every word

The consequences for changing what God has already established as standard. (cf. Revelation 22:18; Deuteronomy 12:32; Proverbs 30:5,6).

of God is flawless; He is a shield to those who take refuge in Him. Do not add to His words, or He will rebuke you and prove you a liar." Proverbs 30:5-6 New International Version (NIV)

To believe in God does not imply to simply accept the existence of God. Rather, it means to see things God's way. One cannot say that he or she believes in God and operates outside God's will. One who believes does as He has prescribed to those who have lived for Him generations before us.

The Effects of Christianity on Believers

10 Christianity is first what happens for you by the cross and then what must happen through you by the cross.

Jesus died to reconcile us with God. Before that, humankind lost its identity followed by the ability to experience life as it was meant to be. Of course, all the blessings of God remained for everyone to benefit from. But the abundant life, the supreme joy, and the sense of fulfillment that can only be achieved with a close relationship with the Supreme Being was missing. Therefore, humankind has long plunged itself into worthless accomplishments while trying to regain the true value lost through disobedience.

Nothing we do can bring us true joy and fulfillment. However, being identified with God fulfills us without any movement. We need to do nothing to be like God; we simply need to submit ourselves to Him. Yes, all we need to do to feel

-10-

His workmanship created for doings good works for the kingdom of God- **Cf. Ephesians 2:10**

The state of being **righteous** *has to do with setting up an example, so others may be inspired by your great new living-Cf.* **Titus 2:1-5**

Complete change to newness of life is required for one who has accepted Jesus and been baptized as His new disciple- **Cf. Romans 6:4**

A public confession is a confirmation that the individual confessed has chosen to walk with Christ- Cf. **Matthew 10:32-33; Mark 8:38**

satisfied in life is to simply glorify the true and living God. To glorify the living God is the only action required from us to access all the power vested in us since creation. Although this seems simple, it is, however, where humankind has failed. For to glorify God means one must coordinate his or her free will to that of the living God. It means that one needs to know what God wants in every aspect of life and to live accordingly.

Why Submit Our Free Will to God?

11 We do not know all there is to know about God's plan for us. And our free will got us in trouble when we used it to disobey God. So it is only wise that, before we do something that may be against the will of God, we check with Him in His Word or through prayer to know what we ought to do, especially before making important decisions.

God doesn't just have good intentions for us. He has a plan for everyone on the planet. He knows us by name. He gave us this free will, and giving it back to Him is a testament to our trust in Him. And trusting God is what true believers do.

Other benefits that come with submitting our free will to God include His favor. As it is written, "Delight yourself in the Lord, and He will grant you the desires of your heart." It also says all things work together for good for those who love God. And somewhere else it says, "if you love me you must keep my commandments." John 14:15 (NIV). Based on these few portions of scripture, it is beneficial for

-11-

Making God in charge of your life- Submit your will to God and He will lift you up in due time- Cf. 1 Peter 5:6

Man's righteous living before God is filthy rags, for no man is found righteous within himself. (cf. Romans 12:2).

Delight yourself in the Lord... Psalm 37:4

All things work together for good... Romans 8:28

If you love me you must keep... John 14:15

Doing all things according to God's will, having Jesus as the perfect example, who has done nothing but the will of His Father; and others, like the apostle Paul and King David (cf. Luke 22:42; Mark 3:35; Acts 12:7–14; Psalm 40:8).

Knowing the perfect will of God by submitting yourself complete to finding His way, turning away from the world and all its perversions (cf. Romans 12:2).

To glorify God: To say to do the will of God as Jesus put it. You give glory to God when you accomplish His will in your life, completing the work He has given you to do (cf. John 17:4).

someone to consider submitting his or her free will to God. Not only is He the best counselor there is, He will also work things together in your favor simply because you consider Him in your decisions.

It is wise to base our last words and final decisions on the Word of God. We cannot be ignorant of the fact that there is an opposing force to our good will, and we may be under the influence of evil and powered by our emotions at times. Our sense of judgment is not always the clearest since we are emotionally unstable. As it is written, "...human anger does not produce the righteousness that God desires." James 1:20 (NIV). The same is true when we are happy; we may do crazy things that are contrary to what God desires us to do. Evil is the nature of humankind, so we are more apt to do bad than good. Those who deny evil's influence in their lives take it upon themselves to do evil and even take credit for it. Pride makes us think we are in charge, but we are all under the influence of evil. We'd like to think we are responsible, and we are, but that sense of responsibility is best used by making the most important decision to submit our free wills under the authority of the high wisdom of God. This way we will be confident in our judgment to choose right over wrong.

The Two Main Aspects of the Christian Faith

12 Essentially, there are two main aspects about the Christian faith to consider. First, we have the spiritual aspect and then the practical aspect of the entire Christian belief. The spiritual aspect is that part of the believer's life that involves personal salvation and how the individual is transformed from the old nature to the new person resembling Christ. Being a Christian is to live a Christlike life. When you have just become a believer, you are not too responsible for your development in the belief. You have the Holy Spirit to guide you in your new Christian life to guarantee that you have the basic knowledge necessary to grow your faith. This may be fulfilled by the support of more mature believers around you or by reading a book, like this one. The spirit of God will guide in acquiring the knowledge you need to grow in the person of Jesus. You, however, need to separate yourself from the company of old friends, and surround yourself with new Christian friends who are mature in the Word of God.

Once you have acquired the basic knowledge, you will come to the point where you must apply that knowledge in your life. That part is the practical aspect of Christian life. All believers struggle with this every day. Although we're still guided by the Holy Spirit, we now are responsible for walking the walk of being a Christian. To be a Christian requires constant work on your character through all kind of circumstances to become a faithful ambassador for Christ in the world. There will be many misunderstandings about you, but God will hold the truth about where you are with Him. You will also hold that truth.

SECTION 2

◆ The Spiritual Aspects of Divine Faith

[Faith is not simply a belief that there is a God or not. Rather, it is a certainty, an inner proof, of a hope that something better must be behind the craziness of everyday life.]

Chapter Contents

The Seven Essential Truths

13 Believers must go through the spiritual process of the Christian faith to be considered a true follower of Christ. This aspect in the life of a believer constitutes a few steps that are fundamental for anyone to be able to become a fervent disciple of Jesus Christ. It is a onetime decision but an ongoing process. And although no one is perfect and all have sinned, anyone serious about leading a Christian life and getting the complete benefit of the greatest opportunity offered to humankind must go through this life-changing process

Part 1

Salvation

Salvation is the act of being delivered from the principal consequence of original sin. Although the act of "salvation" requires that God forgave our sins, the word itself is not to be considered a synonym for the word "forgiveness." Salvation is a greater act than forgiveness. By being saved, we are once again made one with God, through His Son Jesus, whose sacrifice on the cross made the union between God and us possible. The original consequence of the original sin is spiritual death. That is a separation of humankind from God. That separation manifests into all kinds of human difficulties and misery. Salvation has vanquished all those difficulties and put us back in His glory.

What Is Heaven, or the Kingdom of God, and Who Will Make It There?

14 There are lots to say about the kingdom of God and those who will inherit an eternal spot in it. Many will tell about what their religions have settled as the

Topical biblical references: Chose your favorite Bible version to check the following references. The NIV is personally recommended.

-14-

What is the kingdom of God? (cf. Romans 14:17; Luke 13:18–19; Mark 4:26–29; Luke 17:21; Matthew 13:33; 13:44; Revelation 11:15; Daniel 2:44).

The second coming of Jesus (cf. 1 Thessalonians 4:16–17; John 14:3; Philippians 3:20; Colossians 4:3; 1 Thessalonians 3:13; 1 John 3:2).

The way that leads to heaven (cf. John 17:3; 3:37; Matthew 7:21–23; John 14:6; Acts 4:12; John 3:16; Matthew 7:13–14; Ephesians 2:8–9; Romans 10:9; John 3:3; Luke 13:5).

Heaven as described (cf. 1 Corinthians 2:9; Revelation 22:1–5; Hebrew 11:16; John 14:2–3; Revelation 21:1; 2 Peter 3:13).

Time limit for us to live in heaven (cf. Revelation 20:6).

The presence of God (cf. Psalm 15:1–5; 16:11; Exodus 33:14; Revelation 21:22; Psalm 65:4; 1 Kings 8:10–11; Exodus 3:2; Revelation 21:3; Hebrews 9:24; Genesis 14:16).

The New Jerusalem (cf. Revelation 21:1–27; 3:12; Hebrews 12:22; Daniel 12:1–3; 2:44)

way to heaven, and some will even tell you heaven is here on earth. However, the Bible is clear in its explanation of what heaven and the kingdom of God is like. Jesus described heaven as both a place and a concept.

It is important to all who aspire to go to heaven to know exactly what it is like. God, whose property heaven is, does not intend for anyone who shows interest in the place to not clearly know what it is all about. And the church, considered the assigned real estate agent, is not always clear in describing it to humankind, the only prospective clients. But God does not intend to conceal the truth about His kingdom. The Almighty tells us much about both heaven and His kingdom in His Word, which we all refer to as the Bible.

Heaven is not a place created or intended for humankind to live. Heaven is certainly the absence of all the miseries and troubles we experience on earth. It is both the presence of God and the place with streets of gold and the gate of pearls as described in the Bible. We will be very comfortable in heaven. For those of us who make it, heaven is an incredible place and an unbelievable experience. But it is only a temporary residence for those who believe and follow Christ and are part of the first resurrection in the second coming of Jesus. The Bible indicates that those who will make it to heaven will only be there for a thousand years. Our permanent place of residence will be New Jerusalem.

Heaven is a place made for spirits. It's the realm of God and His angels that are there to serve Him. By this we mean the physical place of heaven. Conceptual heaven is the presence of God. Everywhere God is present is heaven. This is the same as paradise. When Adam and Eve were in the garden, before they sinned against God, they were said to have been in paradise. This word "paradise" is mentioned just three times in the Bible. Each time it is descriptive of an earthly place, a place with the aspect of heaven, and not the actual place where God lives. Therefore, it is best to say that paradise is simply the presence of God, wherever it may be.

New Jerusalem, however, will be the new earth, where humankind will live after they spending a thousand years in the habitat of God. Those who are saved, meaning those who didn't burn in the lake of fire—known as hell—with Lucifer, the devils, and all his angels and demons. Those people who are saved will live in New Jerusalem just like it was at the beginning, before Adam and Eve sinned. There we will be forever in the presence of God, just as it was meant to be.

How Does One Become Part of This New Life and the New Earth?

15 The Bible explains how anyone can take part in the kingdom of God and set foot in heaven. There are many approaches to the answer of this question and different kinds of explanations, based on the many different church denominations. But you'll hear only one correct biblical answer from any well-versed Bible scholar you would talk to. The two divine requirements

-15-

*The repentance of your sins-*Cf. Acts 3:19; 1 John 1:9; Romans 10:9; Isaiah 59; Leviticus 26:41-42; Deuteronomy 30:1-3; Isaiah 55:7

*To have zeal and perseverance-*Cf. 2 Thessalonians 3:13; Titus 2:14; Romans 12:11; 2 Timothy 2:12; Revelation 3:15-16

*The good tree produces good fruits-*Cf. Matthew 7:17; Luke 6:43; Matthew 12:43

*Justification not by faith alone, but also through actions or works of faith-*Cf. James 2:24-25

*Chosen by God and Jesus for good deeds-*Cf. John 15:16

*The works of faith-*Cf. James 2:18; Hebrews 11:1-39

for anyone to go to heaven are repentance and zeal, or perseverance. The key Bible verse that supports this answer is one of the most common ones: "If you confess with your mouth, 'Jesus is Lord,' and believe in your heart that God raised him from the dead, you will be saved" (Romans 10:9).

The confessing part is very clear, but the zeal part is not so clear in that verse. It may not be very clear, but it is there. The zeal is found in the believing in your heart part of the verse. The truth is, anyone who believes in his or her heart will have the zeal to show for that belief. To believe in your heart insinuates that one who believes is a true believer, and all true believers will act on what they truly believe in. A true believer shows zeal. Another verse to support this truth is, "For as the body without the spirit is dead, so faith without works is dead also." (James 2:26 King James Version). You cannot say you have faith and believe in Jesus and not have the actions or deeds to show for it.

God doesn't need your good deeds or zeal to qualify Him as God. Your zeal, however, justifies your faith. As it is written, you will know the tree by its fruit. Jesus said it in the following verses.

> "Likewise, every good tree bears good fruit, but a bad tree bears bad fruit. A good tree cannot bear bad fruit, and a bad tree cannot bear good fruit. Every tree that does not bear good fruit is cut down and thrown into the fire. Thus, by their fruit you will recognize them," (Matthew 7:17)

It is common teaching that we are saved by grace, and that there is nothing we can do to deserve it. Biblically, that is true. It is also true that if we have confessed with our mouths the Lord Jesus and been reconciled with God, we need to justify those actions with many other actions. Another statement from Jesus put it like this: "You did not choose me, but I chose you and appointed you so that you might go and bear fruit—fruit that will last- and so that whatever you ask in my name the Father will give you" (John 15:16).

You'll find many places in the Bible telling of your need to show actions to justify your faith in God and Jesus. Here is another great example.

> "What good is it, my brothers, if someone says he has faith but does not have works? Can that faith save him? If a brother or sister is poorly clothed and lacking in daily food, and one of you says to them, "Go in peace, be warmed and filled," without giving them the things needed for the body, what good is that? So also, faith by itself, if it does not have works, is dead." (James 2:14–24)

The conditions for all to make it to heaven are the same. Although we all may be reconciled with God from different tracts of life, God considered us all sinners. We are all saved by grace, by the sacrifice that Jesus made on the cross at Calvary. And we are also saved by the work of our faith.

-16-

The law of God is in everyone's hearts, making them all believers by nature of conscience. (cf. Romans 2:14).

The rest that Jesus offers (cf. Matthew 11:25–30).

The deceptive lies of the devil: Satan the liar and deceiver (cf. Ephesians 6:11; 2 Timothy 2:26; 2 Thessalonians 2:9–10).

The definition of faith: The substance of things hoped for (cf. Hebrews 11:1).

Lessons from the Text

❖ Heaven can be the habitat of God or anywhere God is present. Heaven the place is not made for humankind to live forever. In the presence of God, however, is where we must dwell always.

❖ There is only one condition to be reconciled with God and make it to heaven, where God lives. You need to confess with your mouth that Jesus is Lord, and believe in your heart that God raised Him from the dead.

❖ Believing in your heart cannot be justified unless one shows actions that may prove his or her faith belief. For faith, as it is written, without works is dead.

Personal Faith Defined

16 There are those who believe in God as to trust Him. Others who do not trust God. But no one can truly claim he or she does not believe in the existence of God.

Everyone is desperately in need of a place where they are problem-free. But such a place does not exist in the world in which we presently live. Death is the only status that guarantees complete rest, but that is only true for those who died in Jesus. Another place of guaranteed rest is salvation, the plan offered by God through Jesus. Matthew 11:28 tells us, "Come to me, all who labor and are heavy laden, and I will give you rest."

The truth is we have already been messed up beyond self-repair. We have been so lost and lied to by the devil that the truth becomes the farthest thing in our reach and our capacity to comprehend. A chance to have hold of a great condition of living that was once ours is offered to us again, but no one is being forced into accepting it. Faith is not simply a belief that there is a God or not. Rather, it is a certainty, an inner proof, of a hope that something better must be behind the craziness of everyday life. Faith is knowing better is to be experienced, and there is more to get out of life than what is made real to us. Not all reality has truth in it, and the truth is not always made real to all people. We are mostly living the lies told us by the devil through the many channels of society. Social deception is the only reality most will ever know. The Word of God, which is the only source of truth for all people, is the way for humankind to experience the truth and not just live the reality in which they find themselves.

The existence of God to all being (cf. Romans 1:18–32; Psalms 14; 53).

The Word of God is truth (cf. Proverbs 30:5).

For anyone to experience the truth about anything in life, it is necessary to practice the Word of God, no matter how awkward the Word may seem and sound. To live the reality we are in, how difficult it might be, we must have put into practice the lies we have been told. The same is true with the truth. It is never enough to only know the truth; we must also practice the truth in our lives to reverse the bad reality and the lies that we experience daily. We must practice the truth of the Word of God to make sense of our lives, or we may simply accept whatever deceptive reality comes our way.

There is a life free of stress, worry, and the many burdens that render human existence difficult. With all the important things we feel we must do, the dreams we need to accomplish, and the façade or image we need to keep, there is no time left for the very reason we are on this planet: to live. Everyone gets to die, and unfortunately for some, death appears to be a blessing, a way out of continuous agony. Sometimes, even those considered successful do not have a clear vision of the purpose of life and often end it. Life is not just waking up every day to accomplish the greatest dreams. Life has a more specific definition than most imagine. Life is to glorify what has brought you into existence.

Life is not about God; you cannot give to God something that has no value to you. Life is about you but only for you to find out who you are, so you may be able to function in your own position and benefit those around you and then God. It is natural to be self-centered, and we need to be. It is wrong, however, to be selfish. For although we are made to love ourselves, we are purposed as well to love others as we love ourselves. Life is first about you and then others and then God. The only cares and concerns the world needs from you are those you would like to have and give to yourself.

God does not care if you love Him if you haven't shown some love to those around you. No one wants from you what you would not be willing to try on yourself. The rule is to do unto others as you would like them to do unto you. Neither life nor faith is about God. Regardless of whether we believe in God, He continues to exist. Life is about knowing who you are in God, so you may be able to use your full potential as the only earthly creation created in His image. You will then be satisfied and content within yourself as the spirit person you are, not regarding possessions or personal accomplishments. If we truly know who we are, we will not be worried about or amazed by our successes.

All of us whose parents are still alive and who have a relationship with them always want to accomplish something that will make them proud. However, our parents may still be proud of us in the process. Most important, we are here to make God proud. We are here to perform some good deeds toward each other and bring glory to Him who gave us life. As it is written, "We are His workmanship, created into good works." Ephesians 2:10 Those in business understand this truth well, but they do it for sordid gain. God commands us to do what is good towards our neighbors, not for what we can get in return, but in reverence to God. So faith is a reassurance of what we hope to become and our personal demonstration of the living God, in whose image we were created.

We All Have Faith

17 Everyone believes in something. The advantage of having a personal faith in Jesus is the fact that it reconciles you with God, the Creator of the universe. When reconciled with God, we again become part of God's original plan for humankind. You may have a great plan for your life, but it is not one that guarantees joy at the end. The plan God has for you is one that not only guarantees real success but will be realized

The abundance of life for good works. (cf. 2 Corinthians 9:8).

For we are his workmanship, created for good works (cf. Ephesians 2:10).

-17-

The ministry of reconciliation (cf. 2 Corinthians 5:17–21).

Total peace of God: "Peace, I leave you," Jesus said (cf. John 14:27).

A plan to prosper (cf. Jeremiah 29:11).

Anxiety-free living, with the promise of a peace that surpasses all understanding (cf. Philippians 4:6–7).

Faith is personal: The person approaching God must believe that God exists and that He is gracious (cf. Hebrews 11:6; James 1:6).

The measures of faith (cf. Romans 12:3).

God does not lie (cf. Numbers 23:19; Titus 1:2; Romans 3:4).

The perfect timing of God: He just want to make sure that you are ready for the moment you've been waiting for. (cf. James 1:3–4).

Special note: Find yourself in God and then give all the glory to God who made you. Who are you?

through faith, not through headaches and worry. Your faith in and knowledge of God, which you will gradually develop, will give you the peace Jesus offered that surpasses all understanding. This is what it says in the Word: "'For I know the plans I have for you,' declares the Lord, 'plans to prosper you and not to harm you, plans to give you hope and a future'" (Jeremiah 29:11).

Jesus also declares this as a provision to those who are reconnected to the Father through Him: "Be anxious for nothing, but in everything by prayer and supplication with thanksgiving let your requests be made known to God. And the peace of God, which surpasses all comprehension, will guard your hearts and your minds in Christ Jesus" (Philippians 4:6–7).

Your plan for your life may not even guarantee success, but it guarantees worry, anxiety, headaches— everything that comes with having a great plan or personal dream. The beauty of being reconciled with God and having personal faith in Jesus is that you will be more confident about what you want to achieve in life. Because your faith is now in the God, to whom nothing is impossible. That, my friend, is solid faith.

A Measure of Faith

Faith is a matter of personal disposition. No one is responsible for anyone else acting in faith. You cannot hold someone else with whom you join faith, responsible for your prayer not being answered. There is no liability involved in joining faith with someone to ask God for something in prayer. In due season, each person will receive the promise of God according to his or her faith. No one is placed in a position to pass blame on other parties involved when personal hopes and prayers are not yet answered. For if God is able and nothing impossible to those who believe, the believer is responsible for having his or her prayers answered. If God is for us, no one can be against us. A portion of scriptures found in Romans 8:31.

It is written that God gives everyone a measure of faith. Which is clearly stated in the book of Romans 12:3 (The English Standard Version). That measure of faith grows in accordance with an individual's experience and relationship with God. Someone who spends a great amount of time reading the Bible and in prayer will have a far better faith experience and relationship with God than someone who does not. One should also be careful about the people they want to join faith with. You want to join your faith with someone who has equal or greater faith than you have.

Time and Circumstances

Don't rush God to get your prayers answered. The Bible declares that "God is not a man that He should lie, nor a son of man, that He should repent.". Numbers 23:19 (NKJV). Therefore, don't be so impatient in your prayers, and keep on reminding God of a promise that He once made to you.

If in your faith walk with God, He promised something to you, God will make certain He fulfill that which he has promised to you. But God in His sovereignty knows what time is best for what to

-18-

The power of the Word to change humankind: There is power in the Word of God (cf. Joshua 1:8; 1 Thessalonians 2:13; 2 Timothy 3:16; Hebrews 4:12; 2 Corinthians 4:3–4).

Focus on the things that are above (cf. Colossians 3:2; 2 Corinthians 4:18; Philippians 3:19).

The tree planted by the water (cf. Psalm 1:1–6; Jeremiah 17:8).

happen. Therefore, do not worry and start doubting in your heart that maybe this or that will not happen. Simply trust God, and in due season, your promise will come through.

Lesson from the Text

❖ You need to be reconciled with God through the sacrifice of Jesus Christ to return to the original plan and the destiny God has for you.

One Message and the Many Prophets

18 There is a lot someone can tell another person to encourage him or her to be successful. However, someone can share words of wisdom from the Word of God that evoke life in another. The difference between life and success is that success is what someone might occasionally experience, but life is a complete state of understanding that does not know failure or defeat. True life has an eternal value. "I have come that they may have life, and have it to the full," Jesus says. John 10:10 New International Version (NIV)

Nowhere in the Bible will anyone find a motivation to succeed in life, at least in the sense of amassing for oneself great earthly treasures. Although great riches are promised to those who believe in God, greater emphasis is always been on spiritual treasures. These greater treasures are the true substance of life and ought to be the focus of all humankind. There is power in the Word of God. All things positive will take anyone to a certain level of success, but only the Word of God gives life to those who put it into practice.

The Message of Repentance

19 The gospel of Jesus consists of a few great key messages. One of them is this, "Repent, for the kingdom of God is near." Logic tells you that anyone will prosper in certain areas if they apply the principles of success particular to those areas. One who is called to be a prophet or messenger of God is called to model success in living the life as lived by Jesus Christ in any area of service. Many prophets of God are called from other professions. God completely removed them from their previous careers and positioned them to be messengers of the gospel of Christ to others. These individuals become dependent on the new profession to which they are called. Though they may have been leaders in their previous careers, they are not to even consider being called by the titles they once had. They are now to be called servants or prophets of God. These individuals now have the duty to lead others in a life purposed for the kingdom of God. They have been called to a new life and purpose.

Another key message of the gospel of Christ is to give up everything. A prophet who has not given anything would not be able to ask anyone to give up anything. What have you given up as a messenger of the gospel? What have you repented from as a believer in the new life?

-19-

The message of repentance (cf. Luke 13:5; 2 Peter 3:9).

The message of complete surrender (cf. Luke 14:33; James 4:7; John 5:30).

Follow those who model great examples (cf. 1 Corinthians 11:1; 1 Peter 2:21; Philippians 3:17).

Giving all for the sacrifice of Jesus (cf. Romans 12:1; Philippians 2:5–8; Ephesians 5:2; 2 Corinthians 9:7).

Not everyone living for the kingdom of God is asked by God to leave a decent job or profession. However, everyone who call themselves Christians must turn away from everything that conflicts with living for God. And anyone who cannot do so is not fit to walk with God. One who is called to preach the new life to others must leave something to follow this new life. Then he or she will be able to ask others to do the same. One cannot lead where the individual has not followed. You must take directions before you can give them. As it written, "A blind person can't lead another blind person, right? Won't they both fall into a ditch?"

It's very important who you let lead you. See what the prophet practices in his or her life to see if the message matches the prophet's life. If not, you may advise the prophet to practice what he or she preaches. The new life is to be preached and modeled before others for we are called not to be the map but the light of the world.

Lessons from the Text

❖ The message of repentance is to be preached and modeled in the life of those called to present it.

❖ You must repent from old ways and give up something to be qualified as a messenger of the gospel of Christ.

❖ One who's still living his or her old ways cannot invite others to live new lives.

Grace

20 Given not by merit but for the sake of rejoicing and to motivate gratefulness toward God. Grace is simply a courteous act of goodwill. Every good thing we experience in our lives is the product of grace. We have done nothing, and we will never have anything that will make us entitled to what God gives us all to enjoy. No amount of money or any accomplishment will provide peace, a great marriage, health, or anything that only God's grace and blessings can provide. God graced us so we may grace others. All living for the kingdom of God must practice the grace of God by first accepting His grace toward us and second, doing good deeds toward others simply out of the kindness of our God-softened hearts. As God does not charge us for what we are clearly convicted of, we are not to convict others for what they have done wrong toward us. Instead, we are to offer them the grace we received from God. Love them for love also derives from grace.

Grace, however, is not free admission. Gratitude is how we pay for any kind of grace we receive from God. All who are beneficiaries of God's grace must repay Him in the form of gratitude. We need to thank God every moment for what He continuously does in our lives. Gratitude, again I say, is the only form of payment to God for all He has done and is doing for us.

Grace is not to be ignored. To act like you don't know or do not understand what God has done for you is being ungrateful toward Him. And you cannot ignore God's blessing and ask for more.

The grace of God in our favor (cf. Titus 2:11; Romans 6:14; Hebrews 4:16; Ephesians 1:7).

Being gracious to others (cf. 1 John 3:17; 4:7; Matthew 9:36; Galatians 3:28).

The sacrifice of Jesus to save us (cf. 1 John 2:2; Romans 5:8; Hebrews 10:12; Isaiah 53:5; 2 Corinthians 5:21).

Giving glory through attitude of gratitude (cf. 1 Thessalonians 5:18; Ephesians 5:20).

Stumping on the blood sacrifice of Jesus (cf. Hebrews 10:26; James 4:17; Hebrews 6:4–6; 1 John 3:4).

The state and condition of man after the fall (cf. Romans 5:12; Isaiah 59:2; Romans 3:23; Psalm 55:15; Romans 5:14, 17).

The greatest act of the grace of God toward all is the sacrifice of Jesus for the redemption of humankind. And that is being ignored by millions every day. We have all lost connection with God, which has caused us a great deal of dissatisfaction. We will never be content, despite all our efforts and hard work. We simply cannot find peace with ourselves. God has made it so we can reconnect with Him. By paying Himself the price for our disobedience towards Him, once again we have access to inner joy, peace, and contentment. This is straight from the God-inspired Newton's third law: From every action, there is an equal and opposite reaction. The Word of God says it like this: "An eye for an eye, and a tooth for a tooth." Also, "All who take the sword will perish by the sword."

When we first sinned against God, we lost all contact with God and our purpose for being. The only way for us to get back on track was for someone who not guilty of the same offense to offer to pay for the sin we committed. And since the penalty of sin is death, someone had to die. Jesus, of all who were qualified from heaven, was the only one willing to pay, so we may find forgiveness and be back on track with our purpose. He came, suffered, and died for our sins. Grace like this should not be ignored, but it is by many. We need to be grateful to God by acknowledging all the blessings that He showers over us daily, and be thankful to Him for being so gracious toward us.

Lesson from the Text

❖ Do not ignore the blessings of God toward you. God forgives sins but not ignorance.

Faith, Righteousness, and Miracles

-21-

21 There is a fine line between what we believe, the things that we do, and the supernatural hand of God. Whatever we believe may change from time to time, and our faith will grow in time. As for miracles, God will always act in ways no one understands. Therefore, everyone experiences the miraculous hand of God every day in the simple act of breathing.

But righteousness is to accept the simple things that God has made us able to do that help our faith grow bigger in Him. It takes faith, a great belief in God, to live according to His righteousness. Every day we experience faith, we live the righteousness of God, and we see the miraculous. God has given us all three so we can feel and experience His presence in our lives. If we consider ourselves as the spirit beings that we are, we will not be so distant in our minds of the manifestations of these three spiritual phenomena. We live not according to the flesh but the spirit. There are many occasions when we don't have the physical capacity to do certain things. Then suddenly, the hope we carry in our spirits enables us to find the physical strength to make it happen. That is faith in action. We were once sinners and destitute people, and now we accept the righteousness of God. Because of that, the enemy has no power to claim or declare any condemnation upon us. We believe in the name of Jesus that despite all that may be evident, that God would make a way for us in some very bad circumstances, and we always come out victoriously. If we consider these things and not be

Counting our blessings (cf. Philippians 4:4; Psalm 103; 1 Thessalonians 5:16–22).

No weapon formed against the believer will prosper (cf. Isaiah 54:17).

Careful not to forget your old victories (cf. Deuteronomy 8:19; 2 Kings 17:38; Deuteronomy 4:9).

Salvation is the greatest miracle of all (cf. Romans 8).

forgetful of them, we have the power to overcome all obstacles that come our way, including the worst we can ever imagine.

Lesson from the Text

❖ We need to focus more on past victories and the miracles God has often performed in our lives. That equips us for present and future miracles we might need in our lives.

The free will of man as it was exercised in the garden of Eden (cf. Genesis 3:17).

Man's sinful desires (cf. Jeremiah 17:9; Ephesians 2:3; James 1:13–15; Galatians 5:16, 17, 19–21; 1 Corinthians 10:13).

The justice of God (cf. 1 Isaiah 30:18; Leviticus 19:15; Romans 2:11).

All have sinned (cf. Romans 3:23; 1 John 1:8).

The power of free will or volition (cf. Romans 12:21; 1 John 3:10; James 4:7).

The provision of God for our sins (cf. 1 John 1:9; Romans 6:23).

Submitting to the perfect will of God (cf. 1 Peter 4:19; Ephesians 5:17; 1 Peter 3:17; Romans 8:14).

Part 2

Redemption

Redemption is the act of restoring something or someone to its original state. A price and efforts must be made to render this type of transaction possible. In this case, Jesus has suffered great humiliation, physical pain beyond human capacity, and death to redeem humankind from hell back to the presence of God. The penalty placed on the account of humankind was to be paid by the sacrifice of innocent blood. Jesus was the only one qualified and willing to pay such a tremendous price.

The Cost of Having a Free Will

22 God let people be. And after they do freely whatever they have chosen to do and face the consequences of their choices, they blame God. How can a loving God let such a bad situation happen? The answer is the same God who let you be. God is only responsible for those who have chosen to live according to His Word and follow His principles. He

43

The flesh desires differently than the spirit (cf. Galatians 5:24; Romans 8:5, 7–9; 1 John 2:16).

is only responsible to make happen in your life all He promised you in His Word.

God is also the God of justice. He is responsible for the execution of recompense and retribution in the entire universe. Yes, the Creator is responsible for making sure that everyone gets what they deserve. The only problem is that no one seems to realize that after the fall of humankind in the garden, no one deserves anything good from God. We have all fallen under and then become recipients of His loving grace. We have all gotten the death penalty for wrongfully using our free will to commit turpitude toward the same God who gave us the free will to begin with.

When bad things happen, we start asking why. Every day we open doors to let the devil execute in our lives our worst nightmares by using our free wills. Free will is our ticket to make good and evil happen on earth. The power to decide for yourself is like a double-edge sword. Through your free will, you make good and bad choices. We tend to take credit for being rewarded for the good decisions we make. When the consequences for the bad ones arrive, we say, "Oh, my God," as if God is responsible for all the evil on earth.

In case you didn't know. God is a good God. He protects and loves us. He so loves us that He has made provisions every time we use our free wills wrongfully to find forgiveness for it. Although it was a high price to pay for such a provision, He did it for us anyway.

The only way for us to avoid self-induced troubles and heartaches is to submit our free wills back to God, and let Him dictate His decisions in our lives.

But we so much like to make our own decisions, although we often make the wrong ones. It is the best decision for all who ever made a bad decision and had to pay a great price for it to let God decide for you. It's simple. The next time you come to making a great decision, ask yourself, "What does the Word of God tell us to do in this particular situation?" Stop using your free will all the time. It's not like you know how to use it anyway.

We All Are Sinners

23 We are not to wrestle against flesh and blood. The flesh has its own desires, which are different than those of the spirit. Although we mean well, we all do things that are contrary to what we believe in and that are against our spirits. It might be different from person to person, or one gender to the other, but we are all weak when it comes to things of the flesh. All flesh desires the same things, so no one is exempt of this truth. A woman may have different areas of weakness than a man, but we all have areas of weakness.

The best policy regarding sin is to avoid temptation. It is far better and easier to avoid temptation than to resist temptation. However, temptations come in all shapes and forms. All temptations are for one purpose alone—to get us off God's secured plan. Again, we may not be motivated by the same wrongful desires, but all flesh is moved by something or a few things that are not so pleasant to God. Our closeness to God diminishes our sinful desires to some extent. But if we

-23-

Resist the devil (cf. 1 Peter 5:8; Ephesians 6:10–18; James 4:7–8; 2 Corinthians 2:11; 10:3–5).

Joining near to God (cf. Hebrews 10:22; Psalm 145:18; Zechariah 1:3; James 4:8).

The sinful nature of humankind (cf. Ecclesiastes 7:20; Genesis 8:21; 6:5; Romans 7:17).

No temptation is above us (cf. Romans 13:14; 1 Corinthians 15:33; 16:13–14; 1 John 5:4; 1 Corinthians 10:13).

-24-

The path of destruction. (cf. Matthew 7:13; 1 Corinthians 6:12; Revelation 21:8; Proverbs 3:5–6).

The lust of our hearths (cf. Colossians 3:5; 2 Timothy 2:22; 1 Peter 2:11; Mark 7:20–23).

The power of seduction (cf. Revelation 2:20; Proverbs 7:5; Job 31:1; Proverbs 4:23; 6:25; 1 Corinthians 7:2; 2 Corinthians 11:3).

The deadly consequences of sin (cf. Genesis 2:17; Isaiah 59:2; 64:7; Genesis 3:23; Luke 16:25–26).

Keeping our eyes on Jesus (cf. Hebrews 12:1-2).

still in the flesh, we will always have the motivation to sin against God. The Creator of all things has condemned the sinful nature in us. We need to stay close to Him to lessen our natural penchant to do what is evil.

Dealing with the World's Perversions

24 We suffer in the flesh because many of us submit ourselves to the forces of evil spirits to lead others onto the path of destruction. The greatest force against all humanity is lust, and the greatest weapon in the same category is seduction. Someone is always willing to place before someone else something or certain situations to stimulate an ungodly desire. One needs to be fully satisfied to escape all the traps that are set to make us fall. To avoid temptation, one must find pleasure in the things of the spirit and completely kill the flesh desires.

It is not that we don't have provisions for when we fall into the temptations. But the consequences and the absence of peace that result from falling is not worth the fall. Everything that is against the will of God is hard on the spirit of humankind, and although God forgives us, the confusion we experience walking the path of destruction takes a big toll on us. Sometimes, the pain and consequences are permanent. It is not fun to disobey God. No seduction is worth it if we truly understand the purpose behind it. God wants us to focus on life, but the enemy wants us to choose death. The way to avoid the trick of the enemy is to trust in God's plan and know it well. The greatest power the enemy has on us is our lack of attention. We are not to keep fighting temptations; we are to focus on the plan of God as if there was nothing else for us. We will not be tricked by a fake if we are familiar with the real thing. And there is no way of you knowing the real thing unless you are constantly in it. Therefore, we need to draw near to God and His plan for us, and away from the devil and all his tricks to destroy us. Avoid temptations every chance you have.

> Therefore, submit to God. Resist the devil and he will flee from you. Draw near to God and He will draw near to you. Cleanse your hands, you sinners; and purify your hearts, you double-minded. Lament and mourn and weep! Let your laughter be turned to mourning and your joy to gloom. Humble yourselves in the sight of the Lord, and He will lift you up. (James 4:7–10)

Faith and the Origin of Death

25 Error is human nature. Our wrongdoings, or what we call trespasses, do not affect our relationship with God as long as we recognize our faults and ask Him to forgive us. Although consequences are attached to each of our mistakes, God does not charge us with the errors we make. The only action of humankind that makes a negative impact on our relationship with God is disobeying the Word of

-25-

Nothing can separate humankind from God (cf. Ephesians 3:16–21; Romans 8:38–39).

The stubbornness of humankind (cf. Romans 2:5; 1 Corinthians 5:1–5; 2 Corinthians 12:2–21; Romans 2:8–16; 10:1–4).

True blessings and satisfaction (cf. John 10:10; Proverbs 19:23; 14:1–19; Jeremiah 31:14–16; Isaiah 58:11).

The practice of the Word of God (cf. John 17:17; Romans 10:17; Luke 11:28; Ephesians 6:17; Matthew 24:35; Psalm 119:11; James 1:22).

God. If you harden your neck and decide to do what you know in your spirit is wrong, you have chosen what in the Bible is known as spiritual death. That is a complete separation between you and God. That same separation also excludes you not of His blessings but most definitely of His promises to have a fulfilled life. You will probably have a lot to enjoy but not the peace of mind and spirit you need to enjoy it.

It is by faith, or confidence in the Word of God, that everyone can find the true joy of life. It is in the method, the exercise, and the practice of the Word that life is. And it is everyone's responsibility to teach and demonstrate the ways of God. That is also the will of God for all of humanity to live by.

Part 3

Formation

In the sense of development, formation means to prepare something to make it ready to go somewhere. To educate. To shape in a particular way for a specific line of service. Some have received their formation in school, and some from life. The best formation is that which is divine.

Importance of a Good Formation

26 What is more important than all the effort one makes toward the accomplishment of anything is the motive and belief system that support the accomplishment.

It is a joy to say you believe in God and will do great things in His name. But it all means nothing if the concept you have of God is false, and you know not what pleases Him. Many operate in the Christian faith with a false belief.

Topical biblical references: *Choose your favorite Bible version to check the following references. The NIV is personally recommended.*

-26-

The twisting of the Word of God? (cf. 2 Peter 3:16).

False beliefs (cf. Matthew 7:15–20; 1 John 4:1; 2 John 1:9–11; 2 Corinthians 11:14; 1 Timothy 4:1; John 14:6; 2 John 1:10–11; Mark 7:7; Galatians 1:8; 2 Peter 2:1; 2 Timothy 4:3–4; Romans 10:23).

-27- A New Creation in Jesus Is Necessary

Come you all (cf.
Matthew 11:28;
Isaiah 55:1; John 3:16;
Revelation 22:17; Isaiah
1:18).

A new creation
in Christ (cf. 2
Corinthians 5:17).

To be renewed (cf.
Ephesians 4:22;
Galatians 2:20; 2
Corinthians 5:17).

27 Everyone comes to Jesus as they are. It is a divine obligation for all who are called to the kingdom to renew their minds to the person of Christ to fully benefit from that experience. A person's mentality is made by information received as a child and throughout the course of life. One does not have to be a psychologist to realize that people can be deranged in how they see things and deal with others based on the way they were raised and their experiences in life.

The person of Jesus is a universal mentality. The renewing of the mind to this mentality helps everyone understand the person created by God and the expectations the Creator has for each one, particularly regarding God and then others and then themselves. There is a definite understanding for every aspect of life. However, the enemy will confuse the world in all those aspects to place humankind on a different path from the one intended by God. Our experiences and the information we received certainly made us who we are. The knowledge of God will transform us to the person we ought to become.

-28-

The presence of evil
in the world (cf. John
10:10).

To be made sinners
(cf. Romans 5:19; 3:10;
Psalm 51:8).

Life Is a Struggle

28 The moment we are conceived, we begin dealing with situations that aim to destroy us. Some children are not even born because the conditions in which they were conceived did not expect them. The destiny of those children becomes at risk in the very place where they should be the most secure. Other children who were wanted had their own risks and struggles to deal with. They have doctors who may see what for them are abnormalities and advise their mothers to abort. Other dangers of conception may cause them to be stillborn or cause their mothers' deaths; they will have their entire lives to deal with such an ordeal.

It was a joyous day when many of us were welcomed on this earth. Our anxious parents made the greatest preparations for us, together with others who well know the struggle we have before us in this journey called life. They looked at us as babies with great smiles on their faces and joy in their hearts, happy we were here with them. It is unusual for anyone to feel sorry for a newborn child who has an excellent birth and whose parents are very happy to have that child. Everyone else shares the parents' happiness for a newborn who came without any problems or complications. No one has sympathy for newborn children simply because of the journey they have before them. The reason is because most of us choose to look at the promises and not the inevitable struggles. We were created by God to live a marvelous life, but then the enemy came and changed the plan. We had the promises before we had the curses. All the struggles in our journey do not affect us as long as we keep our eyes on the promises of God, which is the real plan. The sole purpose of the struggles we have is to deviate and blind us to the promises and abundant life that the Creator God has for us.

Every day is a struggle. Every day is also a chance to experience and live the blessing of God. However, for anyone to bypass the struggles and live the life that

Be good onto all-Cf. Galatians 6:10

In all things, be grateful-Cf. 1 Thessalonian 5:18

The plan of God for those who love Him-Cf. Romans 8:28

God is able-Cf. 2 Corinthians 9:8; Philippians 4:19

All good gifts come from God-Cf. James 1:17

God intended, he or she needs the knowledge of God to defeat the tricks of the enemy. When the entire world is filled with lies, deceptions, insults, and false declarations, someone needs to be confident in the truth and constantly focus on it to fight against the struggles. Many will try every day to tell you and prove to you the opposite of what God says. That is very unfortunate. The greatest disadvantage is that many have no idea of what God says and the plan He made for them. The fact that someone doesn't know the own divine truth about the individual's destiny makes it extremely difficult to reach that divine destiny, if possible at all. And being oblivious to your God given destiny is a great opportunity for anyone to lie to you about what you might become. Life is a struggle. This is one of the enemy's deceptions to blind you to your rightful peace of mind and divine promise of prosperity. It is only a reality due to our disobedience toward God and humankind's ignorance in the knowledge of God. For the wise, what is described as struggle to many is simply an opportunity to thrive in difficult moment and to build character. This is in fact what makes the difference between the many personalities you may encounter in all societies. A few among the many personalities are those who complain, those who make things happen, and those who endure whatever happens. Also, you have those who cheat, and those who remain honest no matter how difficult things may get. If there is to be any struggle it should not be life itself, rather it must be a strong resistance towards wrongful thinking that in return would prevent bad intentions towards one another.

Spirit-Filled Advice about Wrongful Thinking

It is a grave danger to a successful life to have the wrong thinking about who one is and his or her purpose in life. Many will try to determine who you need to be based on their perceptions and knowledge. However, God determined who you are before you were born. Most of us have bought the lies from others about our destinies, and our ways of thinking have taken us on different routes. Someone comes to you and says you are this or that. If it sounds somehow negative or even limited, that perception of you is no way from God. You must then go to your God-inspired Christian Bible and find out about yourself. Briefly, this is who the Bible says you are in Genesis 1:27: "God created mankind in his own image, in the image of God he created them; male and female he created them."

This means that, using your God-given talents, you can achieve any level of success anyone else has. For you, too, were created in the image of God with a divine ability to achieve great things.

When you find yourself a bit confused or troubled, try doing these things.

1. Focus on the positive things in your life; in other words, count your blessings.
2. Do something great for someone else.
3. Forgive in your heart someone who has wronged you.

4. Find hope in the Word of God. Read the first couple chapters of the book of Hebrews in your Bible.

-29-

The knowledge that has the power to change your heart-Cf. Hebrew 4:12; Proverbs 3:5-6

Be aware of empty words-Cf. Colossians 2:8

Twisted truths-Cf. 2 Peter 3:15-16

A World of Deceptive Knowledge

29 It's a noisy world. Everyone has something to say. Many communicate what seems to be real knowledge but has no power to change hearts. Knowledge that leads to incomplete success is not the kind of a knowledge you should occupy your mind with. True knowledge will change someone's life, and perfect knowledge produces life. The Bible is perfect knowledge. The many types of knowledge used to motivate humankind to an unreal success take us away from the true knowledge of the Word of God that produces life. Any type of knowledge that exalts itself against the true knowledge found in the Word of God should be condemned. And those professing an empty knowledge that sounds real are all deceivers. The devil is the great deceiver. In the realm of the spirit, Lucifer, who is the angel known as Satan, does not always tell a complete lie but often simply twists the truth.

Spirit-Filled Advice about False Knowledge

Any knowledge being exalted against the true knowledge of God is false knowledge, and its purpose is to deviate people from the truth. False knowledge is being taught everywhere, not just on Facebook

-30-

Ever-learning fools
(cf. 2 Timothy 3:7).

Deceptive knowledge
(cf. 2 Corinthians
10:5).

and other forms of social media. Even in our great universities, students are being taught big lies. For example, they're learning about evolution as opposed to creation. Others include one by Douglas Labier, PhD, that states having an affair outside marriage can be psychologically heathy. Others claim it can even better your marriage. Dr. Labier is a highly positioned member in the world of higher education. However, his knowledge in this domain, based on the ancient truth of the Bible is false. Others, like Dr. Michael Formica, make similar statements about marriage and extramarital affairs. These types of knowledge, although coming from credible members of our society, must be rejected. They can only cause you great misfortune.

Here are some hints about finding truth.

1. The truth frees your spirit.
2. The truth is universal. It does not take sides, and it is timeless.
3. The truth places you in bondage to do good.
4. The truth comforts you and gives you peace.

The Concept of Education as a Higher Calling

30 People learn. However, based on the Christian Bible, there is such a thing as excessive learning without effectiveness. Knowledge is key, and it is acquired by education. But it is acquired also through experience. There are plenty of institutions in the business of offering systemic lines of instruction and make themselves authorities in the domain as if they were the only sources of knowledge. These institutions are responsible for the professional deviation of many individuals and cause great harm to the economies of many nations. Education is key to success, but what kind of education are you receiving?

Any knowledge that is raised above the knowledge of God is demonic. No one is called to education. Everyone is called to service to one another, and education is only one tool used to reach a great standard of service. It is not the education that we must focus on for some are born with talents no one with a formal education can compete with. Some things cannot be taught. For example, how do you type faster than someone who has all his fingers, and all you have at your disposal is one toe? There are no schools where you can learn how to type using one toe. (This is the case of a man named Nick Vujicic, who was born without limbs and learned to type with what resembled a toe.) Many individuals have paved the way for others though they had no one to show them how to get there themselves. They reached where they are using their talents and God's inspired knowledge.

Education is not always available. Sometimes you just have to stumble your way to success because no one has been where you are called to go. If many have successfully made it where you want to be, by all means follow their footsteps. But don't feel stuck if you are the first called to reach the level where you want to be. Just follow your spirit.

Spirit-Filled Advice about Education

King Solomon, to whom God gave great wisdom and knowledge, wrote in the book of Proverbs, "Give everything for knowledge." There is no argument that knowledge is important. It is impossible to achieve anything without first acquiring knowledge about what you desire to achieve. However, knowledge is worth nothing unless it is used to help someone. You cannot limit knowledge to simply a stack of information. You must place whatever knowledge you have in a form of practice to give it value. Too many simply attend school, collecting information that is quickly forgotten for lack of use. Do not make education your calling. There is a foundation everyone must have to function in our society, and everyone must achieve that level of education. However, one must not waste precious time collecting what is not relevant to his or her calling in life. As soon as you find out what interest you and how you would like to serve in the world where you are, focus on it. Get all the knowledge you can on what interests you and is relevant to your calling. And do not settle for just having a job. There are many jobs that one can take and perform quite well, but a calling is why you were born. Find that, and make it useful to others.

Here are some useful steps for achieving your calling.

1. Find your own way to success. Ask questions, and dedicate yourself to finding the answers.

-31-

The truth that set you free (cf. John 8:32; Galatians 5:1; 2 Corinthians 3:17; Romans 6:22; John 1:17).

Blessed are those who keep the Word (cf. Luke 11:28; James 1:22; John 14:23–24).

Don't be kept out of the city of the New Jerusalem (cf. Revelation 22:10–15).

Flee the world and its desires (cf. John 2:15–17).

A godly standard yields great blessing (cf. James 1:25).

The just shall live by faith (cf. Hebrews 10:38).

The unlimited resources of God (cf. Matthew 19:26).

2. Educate yourself. Knowledge is at the disposition of those who seek it.

3. Be persistent.

4. Don't be so afraid of failure.

5. Failure is just a sign that you are well on your way to success. Simply see it as a process of elimination.

6. If you must delay, go ahead and delay. Take small steps, but never stop.

7. Work hard and intelligently.

Honor the Truth

31 It is not enough to just know the truth; it is crucial that we also practice it. The purity of heart and the peace that exist in the promises of God can only be experienced by the honor we give to the Word of God through our faithfulness. Not to follow it as if we were under the law, but as the greatest knowledge and wisdom that leads to an abundant life. The Word, as prescribed by God, is not meant to place us in a punitive bondage. Rather, it is to liberate us from the practice of evil that leads to self-destruction. God so loves the world that He gave His Son in sacrifice, so we may be justified and able to be in relation with Him. However, He also gave us His commandments, so we may walk within them, and His knowledge, so we may go against the tricks of the enemy and all evil spirits that stand against the kingdom of God.

The ugliness of the world comes through ignorance of the Word of God and the practice of fleshly desires of our hearts or souls. Life is great when we live by the standard set by God, and genuine peace is always the result of choosing from His provisions. The universe is put together by God. His knowledge allows us to know how to benefit truly from His many blessings. Therefore, one who seeks to live abundantly in all the areas of life needs first to seek His knowledge on how to really be blessed and not simply hold on to the many empty possessions that guarantee no real satisfaction.

The Word of God was revealed through the prophetic ministries of His servants, who testified that the just, or the righteous, will live by faith. This means those who choose to live by the principles of God, the Creator, will prosper in all areas of life. It is not sufficient for children of God to only going through life possessing things and establishing security based only on earthly resources. Rather, they must seek security based on God, who gives and secures all things. One whose financial security and resources are in God has no limit to what he or she can have.

The Word of God is the foundation to everything that matters to humankind. It is in the interest of all to know what it is written to secure the good life, which is only guaranteed by the Creator of all things. Whether it is wealth or health, it is all secured in God's promises.

Spirit-Filled Advice about Truth and Its Practice

The Bible is a practical book that speaks to your spirit and your human intelligence. You cannot literally do all that the Bible tells you to do for many reasons. The Bible is written for all times, but it can be time sensitive. For example, Jesus said to the disciples, "You have heard that it was said, 'Eye for eye, and tooth for tooth. But I tell you, do not resist an evil person. If anyone slaps you on the right cheek, turn to them the other cheek also" (Matthew 5:38–42 NIV).

There was a time when it was permitted to do certain things for it was the time of observance of the law. After Jesus came, he fulfilled the law, and in so doing, we were freed from all the laws of God no one else could follow anyhow. Jesus gave humankind a new law: to love. The bible is also time sensitive in the sense that we cannot pray some of prayers King David prayed to God for his enemies. Neither can we consider our enemies the way the people of the Old Testament used to and were even required to.

Any truth in the Bible that does not contradict the new way of life established by God through Jesus is to be followed literally. There are only a few exceptions. The following portion of scripture for instance, "And if your right hand causes you to stumble, cut it off and throw it away. It is better for you to lose one part of your body than for your whole body to go into hell" (Matthew 5:30 NIV). Remember that the Bible speaks to your spirit, not to your human intelligence. This is merely a spiritual text. Here, Jesus is not asking anyone to cut off a limb, rather, to sacrifice even that which is important to you if it is causing you to miss out on the eternal blessings that are to come. He is saying to choose heaven and avoid hell at all cost. If the way you go about serving others, or your personal way of life does not contradict the established plan of God, you are well on your way to progress. On the other hand, if your personal lifestyle or the way you do business goes against Divine truth, you are well on your way to complete annihilation. As it is written in your Holy Christian Bible: "When the wicked spring as the grass, and when all the workers of iniquity do flourish; it is that they shall be destroyed for ever." Psalm 92:7 King James Version (KJV)

-32-

Topical biblical references: Choose your favorite Bible version to check the following references. The NIV is personally recommended.

The solid foundation of God (cf. Isaiah 28:16; 1 Corinthians 3:11; Matthew 16:18; 7:24; 1 Corinthians 3:10–11

God among us (cf. John 1; John 1:14; Colossians 2:9; 1:15; Ephesians 2:19–22

God speaks to us still (cf. John 8:47; 16:13; Job 33:14; Hebrews 3:15).

Part 4

Foundation

The foundation is the core of what is, the support system upon which the rest is built. In this case, foundation is the belief system upon which are based all actions and reactions. I believe, therefore, I do and react accordingly. My belief is my foundation from which all my accomplishments derive. I am the exact outcome of what I believe.

Christianity

32 It is a joy to say that you believe in God and that you want to do great things in His name, but it all means nothing if the concept you have of God is false. There are many who are operating in the Christian faith with a false belief.

Everything is strong or weak based on its foundation. Christianity is not the first discipline or religion in human history. However, it is the only discipline where there is a supreme, all-powerful God who has demonstrated his presence to His people and physically lived among them to establish the necessary rapport between the people and their God. Christianity is the only religion that implores a living God. The same God who revealed Himself to the ancients still communicates with today's generation. His relationship with His people never changes. Based on that, we can say to be a Christian is to be current in your relationship with your living God. Those who believe in God need to have a clear understanding of how big a God they serve and how to use that power to achieve great things.

Christianity Concerning the Key Aspects of Humanity

33 The effectiveness of the Christian discipline is the reestablishment of the kingdom of God on earth. It is in the reconciliation of humankind to its Creator, as explained in Luke 17. These statements may not mean much to the natural human, but they are keys to the true values of being. There are many aspects of the human life that make it significantly important for individuals to consider a belief system or evaluate their existing ones to make sure that they really benefit from that belief system. If your belief system is made of myths, it is not necessary to even have those beliefs.

A true belief system must consider many serious aspects of human life and have a real provision for each. A true belief system must give perfect knowledge and understanding to life in its entire sense. It must provide a true definition for the things

-33-

The kingdom of God is here (cf. Luke 17:21; Matthew 12:28; John 3:5; Matthew 11:12; Romans 14:17).

The unnecessary or useless beliefs (cf. James 2:20; John 20:29; 2 Timothy 2:14, 23; 1 Corinthians 1:19; 2:1–6).

The perfect truth and knowledge of God (cf. Proverbs 2:6; Hosea 4:6; 2 Samuel 22:31; Psalm 119:105; James 1:21).

Godliness (cf. 1 Timothy 4:7–8; 3:16; 2 Peter 3:11–12; 2 Timothy 3:5; 1 Timothy 6:6).

that are meaningful to all people and assign a definite role of importance for each stage in the life of all individuals. It must present a clear definition of the role of children, adults, and the of older individuals in the last stage of life. It must also present a clear definition for the role of a mother and a father in the human family structure, the role of a friend, and all the members who occupy a place in the society of humankind.

A true belief system also gives a clear definition and understanding of love, success, happiness or joy, and all other aspects that make the human life worth living. The promise of Christianity or godliness as presented in the Bible offers all those things in one simple package called the kingdom of God.

The kingdom of God is the foundation of the belief system of the Christian faith, otherwise known as godliness. It is the blueprint of success for the life of all individuals living on this planet. There is a truth that is applied to everything that exists. And there are many lies about those same things. There is a true meaning and purpose of life, and there is also a false definition of it. There is a purpose and a meaning for all that exist. However, not everyone knows the truth about life and their own purposes for being. So many perish due to a lack knowledge on those matters. Others perish due to their stubbornness in living the lies they have been told about why they are here. No matter how foolish life may seem, or the degree of pain and heartache people may experience while living a false definition of life, their willpower to survive will help them sustain all those bad living conditions. When the pain of living has become so unbearable, and the lies have become truer than the truth itself, some may decide to put an end to their miserable lives. When the deception is too great and the price paid too much for the life one assumed was best, an individual might no longer be able to trust in any belief system. The person may believe the only way to stop the pain is by ceasing to live.

There is a far better solution to misery than suicide. But that fact is easier to conceive or understand when one's mental condition is intact. Once one reaches the point where self-value or consciousness is lost, it might be too late to accept any truth presented to that individual. That's when you need the true strength of a powerful belief system to help renew your mind. Life is real, so your God and your religion need to be.

The Fear of God

34 The most necessary fear is the fear that nobody has, and the absence of that fear makes humankind fearful of everything.

Those who fear God will not fear people or circumstances because they will not want to deal with God, who said not to fear anything. However, those who do not fear God have no real provisions against any other fear. To fear God is not to tremble in His presence but to trust and take seriously every promise He made to us. In every situation, if someone knows and trusts what God has promised, the person

The process of renewing of the mind-Cf. 1 Peter 1:13; Philippians 4:8; Ephesians 4:23; 2 Corinthians 10:5; 2 Corinthians 4:16; Romans 12:2

God is real-Cf. Isaiah 40:28; Isaiah 57:15; 1 John 4:8; Exodus 20; Exodus 19:5; John 1:14

Your religion and doctrine must be real-Cf. James 1:26-27; Ecclesiastes 12:13; Acts 2:44-45

-34-

Wisdom starts with the fear of God-Cf. Proverbs 9:10; Proverbs 8:13; Exodus 20:18-22

To fear and to love God-Cf. Psalm 15:1-5; Psalm 16:11; Exodus 33:14; Revelation 21:22; Psalm 65:4; 1

The fear of men lays a snare-Cf. 1 John 4:18; Genesis 3:8;

will not have any fear of that situation. Fear comes from ignorance and mistrust, and someone who does not know and trust God has a lot to fear. The only fear everyone needs is the fear of God. That fear will settle all the other fears.

Spirit-Filled Advice about Fearing God

To fear God, the Bible says, is the beginning of wisdom. One needs to have the fear of God to stop from doing what is against the natural and spiritual ways of life. Many are fearful of humans, and others are fearful of situations. The fear of God is above all fear in the sense that God's requirements surpass those of humans and are beyond all situations. Those who choose to fear God will not fall under the snares of others. They also reap the blessings that accompany obedience to God.

Here is some very important information about fear and dealing with fear you should know.

1. Fear keeps you from reaching your destiny.
2. Fear is a lack of knowledge and information.
3. Focus more on knowing the will of God and less on your fears.
4. The more you know about God, the less you are fearful of things and situations.
5. Be prudent, but have no fear.

Exercise and Practice

-35-

35 The base foundation of a great relationship with God lies in these two basic principles: believe in the Lord Jesus Christ, and apply the Word of God in your life. The word "practice" indicates or is more likely to be applicable to someone who has completed all the requirements and is now ready to demonstrate learned skills. The word "exercise," on the other hand, indicates specific effort made to achieve a definite goal. Although the same Greek word (άσκηση) is used to define the two words, the exercise is more suitable for someone who desires to benefit from being in a relationship with God. The Christian life is a practice that can only be achieved through a lot of exercise.

One who has been reconciled with God needs plenty of exercise in many areas to be pleasant to He who created us. God loves us. The only setback in our Father and children relationship with the Almighty is our rebellious ways. God has set things to be done a certain way, and we trust our hearts to the enemy, who advises us to go different ways. It is often not what we want but how we want to achieve it that is against the perfect will of God. We must always exercise our faith and practice the righteousness of God, so we may continuously be in the perfect will of God.

Faith and Exercises

36 The Bible is an active and living book. Everyone who practices the lifestyle and the wisdom prescribed

The exercise of your faith- 2 Corinthians 5:7; 2 Timothy 4:7; Ephesians 6:16; James 1:3; 1 Corinthians 16:13; Romans 1:17

Practice righteousness-Cf. Matthew 5:20; Romans 4:3; 1 John 3:10;1 John 3:7; Romans 6:16; Matthew 5:6

-36-

The active and living book- Cf. Hebrews 4:12

To live the word is its sole benefits-Cf. Revelation 20:6; Proverbs 2:3-5; Proverbs 24:14; Proverbs 8:17-19

The convincing work of the Holy Spirit (cf. John 14:26; 16:8; Acts 1:8; 1 Corinthians 12:13).

Stand for what you preach (cf. James 3:1; 2 Timothy 4:1–2).

by it will experience the best life that anyone may live on this earth and even after death.

The only problem with anyone—whether it is a believer or a nonbeliever—that prevents one from benefiting from the Word of God is the fact that not many put it to practice. No book other than the Holy Bible will ever place in a better perspective the knowledge that God has for humankind to apply in their daily lives. No one's job is to add to the Word of God; neither is it to make anyone understand the Bible. The Holy Spirit is Who reveals God's knowledge to everyone and convinces the people's hearts about what is written in the Word of God. We who are called to teach the Word of God are to help others practice all that is prescribed in it. According to the Oxford Dictionary the word "teach" means "to impart knowledge to or instruct (someone) on how to do something." For example, he taught her to sing; she taught him to ride a bike.

Telling others how to be Christians when we should be examples of that is not teaching. Too many of us want to be teachers when it is not recommended for many of us to do so. As it written: *"Let not many of you become teachers, my brethren, knowing that as such we will incur a stricter judgment." James 3:1 New American Standard Bible (NASB).* If the expression, "Easier said than done," applies to anyone in what they believe in the Word of God, let that person be exempt from teaching others how to apply the principles of the Word of God in their lives. As Jesus said according to Matthew 7:5 (NIV), "You hypocrite, first take the plank out of your own eye, and then you will see clearly to remove the speck from your brother's eye." If you want to teach others how to walk with God, you must yourself be having a good walk with Christ. Otherwise, you risk being called a hypocrite.

This book is not intended to give you additional information about or instructions to God's already prescribed words in the Bible. Rather, it is an exercise book on how to practice the wisdom the Creator has given us. One who is to follow the instructions of God does not need a master's degree or a PhD in divinity. All that are needed is a willing heart and the Holy Spirit to guide him or her. For faith is not a matter of one's intelligence; it is of the spirit of God. One needs to be a disciple and a true servant of God to teach another person how to serve God. Many are called to teach us the Word. However, what you need from them is not the speech from their mouths but their personal testimonies and examples of their own walks with Jesus. You do not need a new word. You need to exercise what is already been planted in you.

A Christian is a faith-active individual who deals with both proactive and retrospective life's circumstances, all according to the Word of God. A true disciple of Jesus is all about exercising and practicing the Word of God. It is logical to say that one needs to know what the Bible says about a situation to apply the Word in that context. Someone needs to clearly know his or her duties as a follower of Christ to be proactive in exercising those duties. You need to know the Word to do the Word. And you need to exercise and practice what you know to be considered a true disciple and servant of God.

A real disciple giving a true example of service to God and others (cf. 2 Timothy 2:15).

The truth that you know will set you free (cf. John 8:31–32).

Blessings and Curses

-37-

God speaks in many ways (cf. Job 33:14–16; Joel 2:28; Hebrews 1:1–2; Daniel 2:19; 1 John 4:1; Daniel 7:1; Deuteronomy 34:10).

Obedience and blessings; disobedience and curses (cf. Deuteronomy 11:26–28).

To live according to the counsel of God (cf. Isaiah 46:10; Romans 15:4; Psalm 16:7).

37 The Bible is the only living proof of a relationship between God and those He calls His children. It contains in those sixty-six books the greatest records and stories of the lives of those who encountered God, the Creator of all things. The Almighty has spoken to many, like Adam, and Moses in the physical realm. However, He is spirit, and so are we. And since we are both spirit beings, we do not need to be in the physical to communicate with each other. God speaks to us in our spirits through our thoughts, dreams, and visions. Although it would be extraordinary for God to come to us in person, no one can deny the presence of God in the spirit, talking to us. When God speaks to us through our minds and spirits, we know that it is Him. You might refer to the experience as your conscience telling you something, but you clearly know that someone in your spirit is talking to you.

In the many encounters God has with His children, He makes a lot of promises that if we act certain ways, it will result in certain blessings. Just like an instruction manual to a vehicle, God gave us directions for using the life He created for us. The same as no one can create life, no other but God, who created life, can tell us how to better live what He created. So we all fall under God's authority to tell us what to do. And as good stewards of a life that was given to us, if we follow well His instructions, we'll reap the blessings that come with our obedience. However, if we choose to go against His directives, we will also reap the rewards or the costs that follow our disobedience. The rewards for our obedience we call divine promises or blessings. For our disobedience, they are called consequences or curses. God's desire is that no one must suffer consequences or curses. For this, He kept the Bible as the greatest written record and examples of those who violated and those who followed His directions. He speaks to us through our minds and spirits to follow the examples of those who obeyed. The Bible is your God-given manual on how to be blessed and to avoid God's curses. It is of the greatest advantage to those who are attached to it, read it, and put it in practice.

Spirit-Filled Advice about Blessings and Curses

It is as simple as basic instruction: do that which is good, and you will reap the reward; do that which is evil, and you will pay the consequences of your willful decision. The truth is God cannot make you do things. As it is written in the book of James chapter 1, starting at verse 13 (KJV), "Let no man say when he is tempted, I am tempted of God: for God cannot be tempted with evil, neither tempteth he any man: But every man is tempted, when he is drawn away of his own lust, and enticed. Then when lust hath conceived, it bringeth forth sin: and sin, when it is finished, bringeth forth death." This cannot be emphasized enough. We are responsible for our own actions. Although we might be influenced by the enemy (the devil) to do evil, it is still up to us to either take or reject the bait he throws at us. We are highly intelligent creatures with the power

-38-

The kingdom of God and definition (cf. Romans 14:17).

to choose between right and wrong. We all know the difference between the two, but we let ourselves be tricked and confused by incentives or short-term rewards that seem to accompany the wrongdoings. While the enemy still exists, there is nothing we can do to avoid being tempted by evil. The best way to fight, as suggested in the Word of God, is not to try to stop evil but to overcome it with good. One will seldom be busy doing both evil and good.

The Kingdom of God

38 Everyone seeks the benefits that come with the kingdom of God. What most people do not want is the authority and person of God that come with the kingdom. The truth is there is not a kingdom without a king. The presence of the king is not to simply make the rules but to guarantee those benefits promised by His kingdom. What benefits are promised by the kingdom of God? What is the kingdom of God as He presents it in the scriptures? It's said in the Bible that the kingdom of God is not eating and drinking. Instead, it is righteousness, peace, and joy.

Who does not seek justice, peace, and joy? In fact, many have risked their lives, leaving their own native lands—including family and friends—for the prospect of finding in foreign places what only the kingdom of God can guarantee. It makes no difference where you are and what physical, mental, or psychological condition you may be in. The kingdom of God is the only place where virtually everyone will experience true joy or happiness.

Part 5

Transformation

Transformation is the act of changing from one state to a better state, becoming anew, and moving from one direction to a better one. Transformation is seen in things and people that have been exposed to that which affects the core of a being. In this case, transformation is the change in a person after being exposed to the true gospel of Jesus. Those who truly understand the Word of God show the evidence by the way they are transformed to better human beings. A true disciple is a transformed individual.

The Perfect Will of God

39 It is written in the Word of God that many are called, but few are chosen. Another passage mentions, "not those who say Lord, Lord, that will enter the kingdom if God but those who do the will of God that will enter."

Many are indeed called into the kingdom of God, and the church is filled with people who call

Many are called but few are chosen-Cf. *Matthew 22:14; Matthew 7:14*

The perfect will of God-Cf. *Romans 12:1-2; 1 John 2:15-17*

To be in the will of God-Cf. *1 Peter 2:15; Ephesians 5:17; 1 John 2:16-17; 1 John 2:28-29*

His workmanship created onto good works-Cf. *Ephesians 2:10*

True joy and satisfaction comes from God-Cf. *Proverbs 10:22 Jeremiah 31:14-16; Isaiah 58:11*

To Bear Fruit Worthy of Righteousness -Cf. *John 15:5; Matthew 3:8; John 15:8*

themselves Christians, followers of Jesus Christ. The matter that is essential to the calling of God to be a disciple is not the act of joining a local church or even in confessing Jesus as a personal Savior. The truth that is essential in being part of the kingdom of heaven is in the practice of the faith and the daily application of what the Word of God says.

As it is written, we are His workmanship, created for good works, and we walk within them. The believer is not one who simply believes. The true believer submits to a relationship with God to find His direction and accomplish His perfect will on this earth. For many, that means to have a world ministry and operate on the greatest scale of service based on the number of individuals served. For others, it may simply be to raise some great children and a family for God. However, for all it is to find peace and be content in knowing Him. No one will ever be satisfied with the level already attained, no matter how great it is. However, one will be satisfied knowing that he or she is in the will of God.

The world is filled with busybodies, furiously trying to advance in life. Many have traveled the road to success for many years. Some have reached great success. But the moment stays with them for a very short time until the stress of getting there and remaining on top steals all the joy out of their success. True success comes in being close and captured by what the truth is in all circumstances of life and to act according to God's Word of God while we are in it. True success is the practice of the righteousness of God. However God tells you to handle the situation is how you will find peace in it.

"Without Me you can do nothing," Jesus said to the disciples. "You did not choose Me, but I chose you and appointed you that you should go and bear fruit, and that your fruit should remain, that whatever you ask the Father in My Name He may give you" (John 15:16 NKJV).

We are not here on this earth to do whatever we want and live our own lives. We are to be connected to God through Jesus Christ and to behave and act like God's children. We were made a success. We are not trying to be a or find success. If we remain in Him just like we are called to do, we will be in perfect peace and live in perfect peace and harmony with ourselves and others. If we are fulfilled in God, we will not have in our hearts the desires to compete or prove ourselves to one another. The spirit of envy cannot manifest in anyone who truly lives in the example of Jesus and be a servant, just like He was a servant to others. If we are truly branches connected to Jesus, the true Vine, we are truly living with divine purpose. We will not be looking to advance ourselves over others or be a pain to others. Instead, we are willing to open our hearts and reflect God to others in how we respond in life's situations and act toward those who might need living testimony of God's love. Our true and divine purpose—the perfect will of God—is for us to identify ourselves in Him. All God's children must resemble Him.

Do Not Love the World

Envy is of the devil, and is also of the fruit of the flesh-Cf. Proverbs 14:30; Proverbs 24:19; Galatians 5:26

The children of God must resemble God (cf. 1 John 3:9, 10; 3 John 11; 1 John 3:6, 7).

-40-

To love the world is to hate God-Cf. 1 John 2:15; 1 John 5:19; James 4:4

The fruit of the spirit (cf. Galatians 5:22–23).

-41-

Those who are following God for food and are servants of their stomachs-Cf. Matthew 4:4; John 6:27; Philippians 3:19

To be broken-Cf. Psalm 34:18; Psalm 51:17; Matthew 5:3

The raffs of men and the justice of God-Cf. James 1:20

The Lord is who must fight your battles (cf. Exodus 14:14).

He who lives under the protection of the Most High (cf. Psalm 91:1).

40 There are practices in the world that do not conform to the principles of God for His children. There are behaviors that are normal to humankind but forbidden by God. These practices and behaviors glorify certain things and not God, so no servant of God should take part in these practices.

The Bible says to get out from among them. This will not be possible technically. However, we are to keep away from the world's activities that displease God. Many of us have the habit of gossiping. We, as Christians, are to condemn such actions. We are not to talk about others as to blemish their good names. Other habits, like the use of foul language, are not to be used by those who call themselves believers. Let nothing you do as a child of God bring shame to His kingdom. We are His righteousness in Christ Jesus and need to serve as good examples for others to follow.

Submit Yourself to God

41 We must know that once we have already known Jesus, nothing will be greater than that experience. No grace will surpass that of being in a good relationship with God, your Creator and Father. The fact that people come to God by accepting Jesus as their personal Savior and have before God the great desire to become anything but good disciples for the kingdom is carnal. We come to God to know Him, not simply for what He can do for us, which He does anyway for those who seek Him.

The greatest inspiration for those who aspire to become the righteousness of God should not be just how many material things they can accumulate as blessings in the kingdom of God. Instead, it should be based on how close to His image they can get. How much we can resemble God is the prime directive for those in Christ.

God has in service many individuals broken in their spirits to share His Word with others whose lives and relationships are broken away from Him. No one can serve God with a self-centered, whole spirit. One has to be first broken and then be made whole in Him to carry out the message of completeness in God through Jesus Christ. One who is still seeking a life and has a personal agenda cannot be a servant of God. The same for a woman who is out to please herself cannot be a good wife. The church is the bride of Jesus Christ, and any individuals or assemblies who claim to be part of the universal church yet live to please themselves is not of God. The devil is selfish and has for servants a world of selfish people who may call themselves members of a church. God's people are well satisfied and content.

The greatest and gravest misconception among people is that when they rebel against what is right, they claim their own rights before whoever established the rules of righteousness. However, what they don't know is that rebellion, which is claiming a right you do not have, automatically makes you lose your divine protection and rights before evil. Being submitted to the will of God keeps you under the protection of God. But if you are out to do your own thing,

-42-

Self-denial for the sake of God (cf. 1 Corinthians 8:8; Matthew 16:24).

Having lost the first love for Jesus and the things of God (cf. Revelation 2:4–5).

God is revealed in His Word (cf. 2 Timothy 3:16–17; John 1:14; Hebrews 1:1–2; 2 Peter 1:21).

The becoming of a whole new man (cf. Ephesians 4:22–24; 1 Corinthians 13:11; Titus 2:7).

God will not be responsible for your defeat. The realm of defeat covers a broader aspect than many think. It may still look like you made your point and were successful being rebellious, but the result of all rebellion against God's ways is destruction.

The Process of Freeing Yourselves from Yourselves

Whosoever wants to be my disciple must deny themselves and take up their cross and follow me.

Mark 8:35

42 Many come to Jesus with a desperate need for Him to be in their lives. After they know Him, some start demanding that Jesus be in their lives what they want Him to be. They had no ideas how to lead their lives in the right direction and get themselves out of the troubles they dug themselves into. However, after they found Jesus and He made them free, they dictated to Him what they wanted. They could not have done it without Jesus. They could not master their own lives and lead themselves out of the problems they were in, but now they wanted to be master over Jesus, the true Master of the universe.

No one will ever be able to guess who they are until God reveals it to them. One who is the master over your life has the God-given knowledge and power to guide you in the direction to become who God wants you to be. Jesus is the only being with that power. He knows where He's taken you from and where God wants to take you. It is not wise trying to interfere with God's plan by being stubborn in your preconceived ideas about your destiny. No one has that knowledge of his or her true destiny unless it is given by God. The best way to find out who you need to be is to first seek God.

The process of freeing yourself from yourself is made real in diligently seeking God. And the way to find God is in His Word. You cannot be looking to know God and not look for Him in the Bible. It is the only book that contains the greatest experiences and testimonies of those who have found Him before you. God is clearly revealed in the Bible.

Everyone should have a profound interest in knowing the person God. No one has a real self-knowledge unless they know the truth about God. The process of freeing yourself from yourself leads the way to knowing who God is. At the end, you will also find out what capacity you have and your true person, which you thought you knew. There is only profit in letting loose of the person you think you are and embracing the real character you ought to be.

The Hearts of Men

There is nothing wrong with the world, but the ignorance and the foolishness in the heart of men.

43 It is written in the Bible that "My people are destroyed for lack of knowledge." It didn't just stop there. The verse continues: "because thou hast rejected knowledge, I will also reject thee, that thou

-43-

The people perished due to the lack of knowledge (cf. Hosea 4:6).

The knowledge of good and evil (cf. Genesis 3:5).

The curse brought to us by Adam (Romans 5:12).

To be like children (cf. Matthew 19:14).

Godliness and having less stuff is a gain (cf. 1 Timothy 6:6–7).

shalt be no priest to me: seeing thou hast forgotten the law of thy God, I will also forget thy children." Hosea 4:6King James Version (KJV)

This is not a matter of not knowing. Rather, it is a matter of rejecting the knowledge to follow your own heart's desire. The consequences that come with that is divine rejection.

The knowledge of right and wrong is in the heart of humankind. The lack of virtue to help them overcome temptations is where most fail. The idea that people are born good is true but based only on the fact that everyone has a conscience, and there is no malice in the heart of a newborn baby. There is no resentment in an infant. Jealousy is not in the hearts of children. Selfishness is the only flaw or wickedness humankind is proven to be born with. Children will tell you, "This is mine." However, they will share with each other in due time. Innocent children only have prejudice against what is fearful and has a bad spirit, which can be psychological or a natural protective feeling to help them protect themselves and stay out of danger. It is normal for a child to not feel too comfortable with a stranger or someone with a mean demeanor. Again, this may be part of the defense system. There are no bad intentions in children. Human nature is good, although humankind has inherited the curse of Adam. Evil comes as we become aware of the difference between good and evil. Then we make the choice to accept one and reject the other.

People become more open and attentive to seductive spirits telling them what to do due to the desires of their hearts. The more desires we have, the more we are open to new knowledge, suggestions, and seductions.

It is recorded in the Bible that all the trouble of humankind started from the desire of the first woman created, Eve. It wasn't wrong that she desired; it was simply wrong that what she desired was forbidden. Although that event greatly cost us, we have followed that same pattern since. We never stopped desiring what is forbidden for us to have. And although the woman was the first seduced to have what was forbidden, we cannot make her the only one responsible, since Adam fell into the same trap. Eve was tempted by the devil, and Adam was tempted by Eve. But in any case, they were both seduced into doing something wrong. Their motives and desires could be different, but they both desired something. The Bible says that Eve desired knowledge. Adam may have desired to please Eve, but a desire is still a desire. Every time we desire something—whether our selfish desire or the desire to please someone who has a desire—we are open to temptations and to doing what is forbidden to fulfill that desire.

The level of godliness or spirituality of a man or a woman is proven by the amount of stuff they have and the purpose behind having them. The less desire for personal things a person has, the more trust he or she is proven to have in God. The transformation of our hearts from being carnally minded to being spiritually minded is the key to be exempt from all evil temptations. And the knowledge of God is how we come to that type of transformation.

The Understanding of Grace and Blessing

-44-

Your delight in the Lord and your heart's desire (cf. Psalm 37:4).

The grace of God is for all humankind, whether you are considered good or evil (cf. Titus 2:11; John 3:16).

Ownership of the kingdom of God through Jesus (cf. Romans 8:17; Titus 3:7).

44 The grace of God falls upon believers as it does upon those who do not believe in God. However, God blesses His children. "The blessing of God makes one rich, and He adds no sorrow with it." *Proverbs 10:22 (NKJV).* God will bless you regardless if you desire anything or not. "The Lord is my Shepard I shall not want." *Psalm 23-28 (KJV).* This word "want" is also translated as "lack." The Lord is your shepherd; you shall not lack. The Bible says that God knows your needs.

He who lives by the river has no need for a big reservoir. As it is written, we are to place our delight in the Lord. We need to make God our joy, and He will give us the desires of our hearts.

There is a great difference between the grace of God and His blessings. Anyone who is breathing experiences some kind of grace from God. Anyone with good knowledge to acquire wealth does it by the grace of God. For it is written that it is God who gives the ability to make wealth. It is a grace from God to have a great spouse, a great family, and fantastic children. But it is a blessing to have peace in your heart with or without any of those things. The grace of God requires not that anyone be deserving of whatever God gives. But to be blessed by God, one needs to do as He says. God's blessing requires that the beneficiary follows His instructions. His grace you will never be able to do anything to deserve, but His blessings come with your ability to listen and do what God tells you to do.

A great example of the grace and the blessing of God is this. Jesus is a grace from God to all humankind. He was sent to us so we may be reconnected to God. We did nothing to deserve that God send His only Son to come, suffer, and die so we may again have personal access to Him. God chose to do that for humanity out of His own good and loving heart. However, salvation and heaven are blessings. One needs to accept Jesus and follow His instructions to be saved from the foolishness of the world and make it to heaven.

"If the Son therefore shall make you free, ye shall be free indeed." John 8:36 King James Version (KJV).

All sort of freedom has been given to humankind. People all over the globe are fighting daily to gain or keep the freedom that God wants them to have. However, in the fight for freedom, many have put themselves in new bondage. Bondage of the spirit cannot be compared with any other type of bondage, whether physical, psychological, or religious. Anything affecting your mind or intellect is nothing compared to what can affect your spirit being or your soul. Whatever force or knowledge that frees you from a previous bondage automatically enslaves you to that new force. Jesus is the only true source of freedom because His knowledge does not make you a slave to Him. Instead, it gives you ownership to the kingdom of God. He makes you as free as He is. However, you are not to be independent of Him. Rather, you will become connected to Him and to God. It is by the grace of God that we have once again become part of His kingdom.

In the light of the Word, Hebrews 10:34 (NIV) says, "You suffered along with those in prison and joyfully accepted the confiscation of your property, because you knew that you yourselves had better and lasting possessions."

The step of transformation stands in the way of many believers and costs them the final reward of being saved. God will not force anyone to enter His kingdom who refuses to rid himself or herself of all old habits. You cannot call yourself a Christian and not value the principles and virtues that make you one. And to show appreciation for God, one must show deep hatred for all that is evil.

Part 6

Revelation

The simplest meaning of this word is knowledge.

The Bible is the greatest source of spiritual revelation known to humankind. The reason is that many examples of those who have walked with God, and who have lived by faith in the Creator, are found in that book. The Bible is the living proof that we are who we are as the spirit being that we are. God's will is that there is continuity in His relationship with us humans. And since many have followed the road of faith in the Creator, He wants us to have knowledge of those individuals and establish a connection with them. There is purpose in the truth of the past—or history, as we call it. Part of that purpose is to help secure the present and plan the future.

The following texts tell us something about ourselves according to the truth of the past as found in the Bible. That will help us understand our true values and the dangers posed against us.

When Evil Rules

Topical biblical references- *Chose your favorite bible version to check the following references. The NIV is personally recommended.*

Testimonies of faith of a few from the many who served before us. *-Cf. Hebrew 11:31-40*

-45-

God revealing Himself to us in His Word-Cf. Mathew 24:35; John 1:1; Hebrew 1:1; 2 Peter 1:21; 2 Timothy 3:16; Deuteronomy 29:29; Proverb 30:5-6; 2 Peter1:23; James 1:21; 1 Samuel 3:21; 1 Samuel 3:7

We are under the empire of the evil one-Cf. 1 John 5:19; Ephesians 6:12; 2 Corinthians 4:4; John 14:30

He who is with us is far greater than he who is in the world-Cf. 1 John 4:4; 1 John 5:4

We are not to wrestle against flesh and blood-Cf. Ephesians 6:12

45 We are under the empire of the evil one according to the Bible. There is nowhere you are where there isn't someone who represents or operates under the influence of evil. Those who serve God are a minority on this earth. Our only advantage as Christians is that we operate under a greater system than the evil ones. "Greater is he that is in you, than he that is in the world." *1 John 4:4 (KJV)*. Thus, according to the words of God the power of good is far greater than the power of evil.

"In the world you will have tribulation;" Jesus said to the disciples. *John 16:33 (NKJV)*. It is very evident that we do. After the fall of Adam and Eve, trouble inhabited the earth. Although we who are in Christ have been redeemed from all the curses that came from our sinful natures, we still have an adversary who has not completely been taken out and off our tails. God, who so loves us, has given us this greatest opportunity to regain our rightful positions on earth. However, Satan, the adversary, will not give us a free pass to the kingdom of God without putting up a fight.

The devil has the entire world targeted. No one is exempt to the deception of the evil one, who wants to make us miss the purpose of our existence. Satan, who was an angel turned evil by his pride, does not accept our position as being closer to God than he is. He could not have defeated God who created him, but he figured he could trick humankind out of the power we have as sons and daughters of God. Let's think. If someone is way too powerful to take his possessions from him, a smart person will try to get them from his children. This is exactly what the devil has done. He could not overthrow God, so he has His children. He is not using his power but that which God gave us to serve each other. Satan cannot use his power to hurt us because, as God's children, we are far more powerful than the devil. Therefore, he uses one person against another and the power of deception to get us away from the divine plan and protection of God.

That power of deception worked on Adam and Eve and is still very effective on us today. The devil is the greatest liar known in both the spirit and the natural realms. He is known as the great deceiver. The devil and those who fall for his deception and submit themselves to his authority are the reasons for all the suffering on earth. Therefore, we ought to be careful how we act toward each other for when we do what is wrong toward others, we submit ourselves to the influence of the evil one to be used by him. All good deeds are inspired by God, and all that is evil are inspired by the devil.

I Have Nothing but God

46 I have gone through my entire life looking to be successful and to prove myself. All without realizing that I have nothing to prove other than being a child of God. By that, everyone will know how important I am really.

It is ludicrous how many individuals live to prove themselves as being a certain nationality and are very proud and forward to claim themselves as such.

Be cautious that we don't destroy one another-Cf. Galatians 5:15; Galatians 5:26

-46-

Humankind is entirely created in the image of God (cf. Genesis 1:26–27; Colossians 1: 15; 2 Corinthians 3:18; 1 Corinthians 11:7; Romans 8:16).

No respect of person before God-Cf. Romans 2:11; 2 Chronicles 19:7

We are not to have respect of person in our judgement-Cf. James 2:1; Mathew 7:12

It is God who gives the power to make wealth-Cf. Deuteronomy 8:18; Proverb 10:22; 1 Timothy 6:17-19

Give all that have for knowledge-Cf. proverb 4:7;

The story of Martha and Mary, and the one who has chosen the better part-Cf. Luke 10:38-42

Without faith it is impossible to please God (cf. Hebrews 11:6),

Some take pride in being part of prestigious clubs and organizations. Meanwhile, they neglect what really makes them the important people they seek to be.

No one will find a greater importance than being identified with God and made in His image. Therefore, everyone is as important as anyone else on earth. I resent the term "VIP." The term implies that there are some who are more important than others. Everyone is important and, therefore, should be treated the same. There is not an instance in life where someone is to be considered less important than anyone else. Not even when someone is lost and has sold his or her soul to the devil. That person is still as important as those of us who have been saved and redeemed. For we were once among their numbers. In fact, it is exactly for such persons that God sent His only Son to suffer and die. We all have the same value in the eyes of God.

I am all sufficient in Jesus, who has reconciled me with God, my Father. And now that I have God, I have all things. However, in all that I have from God through Jesus, there are some that are more important than others. Not all God's blessings have equal value and importance.

God gives the power to make wealth, the Bible says. However, can the devil also give wealth? The answer is yes. The devil will offer everything. He cannot, however, give all things. For example, the devil cannot give peace and security. The devil cannot give or sustain life. The devil can provide money to buy a lot of things, but he cannot guarantee satisfaction.

The greatest gift we have ever received from God is His knowledge. That is of a greater importance than anything else He has given humankind. Without the knowledge of God, the alternative would be a life lived without purpose. God reveals Himself to all his children, and those who haven't considered themselves as such live with a burden inside them to know they are in relation to a higher power and purpose. If the knowledge of God ever comes to you and the true revelation of the creator is ever present before you, please do not ignore it. The only chance for you to truly separate yourself from the rest of the animals is for you to find your divine purpose. Without a revelation from God, everyone is as good as dirt.

The worst thing about having a hunger for something is that you might do stupid things to satisfy it. And at the end, still have that hunger.

Seek God and His knowledge. He will surely reveal Himself to you.

Topical biblical references: Choose your favorite Bible version to check the following references. The NIV is personally recommended.

-47-

To be a witness to the kingdom of God (cf. Acts 1:8; 4:20; 22:15; Matthew 28:18–20).

The trials of our faith are to make us better people (cf. James 1:2–4).

The greatest in the kingdom of God (cf. Matthew 20:26).

To live for the glory of God (1 Corinthians 10:31; 2 Corinthians 3:18).

The call to greatness (cf. Isaiah 40:31; 1 Peter 2:9).

Part 7

Elevation

This is the act of being taken from a lower level and placed at a higher, more dominant level. The action takes one from humiliation to a place of honor. It is to be recognized in a greater dimension. Elevation is a form of promotion.

Instant Calling to Greatness

47 The day you became a disciple of Jesus, you were called to serve others and be a witness to the kingdom of God. The latter means that you have come to experience a better way of life and a better understanding of that which may appear difficult for the ordinary person to comprehend. You have come to a clear understanding of life, the purpose of it and the great knowledge of Divine destiny.

There is a season for everything on the planet. Only one purpose connects all we do and the seasons we do them in. All we have experienced and every season in our lives are to serve one purpose. Although some moments in our lives may be difficult, we are to be strengthened in character and become the best at serving each other. We live to glorify the living God through our services to others. All that does not serve this purpose should not be in the agenda of anyone claiming to be a discipline of Jesus.

The notion that the Christian life is difficult has some truth to it. However, if one works and does everything for the glory of God, that person will find the road of righteousness much easier to travel and much more profitable.

According to the words of Jesus, "come to me all who are tired and weary." The difficulty we have in our walks with Jesus are all due to our stupid desires to live between two worlds, the world of Christianity and the world of rebellion.

God's will is to raise everyone into dignity. It is the will of God for all to find their positions in the kingdom of God. But first, we need to be willing to go through the process of having a change of heart. We also must change our visions and personal ambitions. God desires what is good for the entire world, and if you have complexity in your heart toward different kinds of people, you will not be able to fit into the plan of God. A godly servant is a universal servant.

We the people of God are called to greatness. For it written in 1 Peter 2:9 (NKJV), "you are a chosen generation, a royal priesthood, a holy nation, His own special people, that you may proclaim the praises of Him who called you out of darkness into His marvelous light."

-48-

*The crown of glory (cf.
1 Peter 5:4).*

We are the people of God. We who have His knowledge are to represent Him before those who are seeking to find Him. We must behave as such and be open to perform the work that we have been called to do.

The Only True Purpose in Life

48 The truth is everyone will die. And there is no real purpose in life if death is feared by those who will die.

The greatest fear in death is produced by the fact that the person dying has not lived enough. And although some would live to be a hundred, that fear may still exist if no real purpose has not been fulfilled in their lives.

We are all about the same thing in life, and that is personal satisfaction. Everyone is after something that will make them feel satisfied or happy. So we look after many things that only guarantee moments of pleasures. And although some of those things are in the will of God, they were not designed to provide the kind of satisfaction our inner spirits long after. Whether it is the perfect marriage with the mate of our dreams or having a family that is in the will of God, none of that can fully satisfy. For the most part, those things are considered blessings, and God, in His goodness, pours these kinds of blessings on whosoever. You do not need to be in Jesus to be blessed with money or to have a successful marriage with the spouse of your dreams. And some who are in Jesus do not have the knowledge to be successful in anything. All to say that material blessings and walking with Jesus do not necessarily go hand in hand. Nonetheless, everyone is after what brings them complete satisfaction during this time of their lives.

It is rather godly for all to look after something to satisfy their souls. God has designed it so a living person looks to satisfy his or her soul. This is also the principal reason for many to look for God. The only accomplishment that will satisfy anyone's soul is to be submitted to the sovereign will of God. Therefore, the only questions that remains are: What is the will of God for your life? What has He placed in your heart for you to do for Him?

All that God has placed in your heart to do is His will for your life and contribute to reaching your destiny. Doing the will of God, conforming to the standards and principles prescribed in His Word, will not only please Him but also give you the satisfaction and fulfillment most so look for. And at the end of life, when death comes, you will pass onto eternity with no hard feelings toward anyone, even those who have caused you pain, like Stephen asking God to forgive his persecutors while being stoned to death, or Jesus on the cross. Your soul can be satisfied, regardless how long you lived. Having done his will is the ticket to your greatest reward and satisfaction.

Material blessings are no comparison to being in Jesus (cf. 1 Corinthians 2:9; Philippians 3:8).

Passing unto eternity joyfully (John 11:25–26; Psalm 116:15).

The death of Stephen (cf. Acts 7:54–60).

What is your true mission? (cf. Psalm 96:3; Acts 13:47; Galatians 6:10).

SECTION 3

♦ The Practical Aspects of the Christian Faith

*[Simply believing will not get anyone
from point A to point B.
Faith without taking actions in the
right direction is like idling
of the finest motor vehicle. Great may be the capacity
to take the journey, however, all the precious fuel
has burned, standing in one place.]*

Chapter Contents

The Christian Faith in Relation to the Important Factors of Our World Society

49 This is where we make a difference in the world. World societies do not care that Jesus came and died on the cross if those who belief cannot show the difference in the aspects of life that matter to all. The first believers had the resurrection as evidence to convince others that it is a benefit to those who believe. There is no evidence more convincing than someone raising others and himself from the dead. That should have been enough to convince everyone to join the first crowd who called themselves followers of Christ.

The message of the cross is first spiritual and second practical. Jesus fed those who were hungry, healed those who were sick, and performed miracles that were necessary in getting the attention of those who lived in that time. Today, we believers have demonstrated the same power all over the planet, but prospective believers don't seem to be impressed with the same techniques that Jesus or the first believers used to convince potential converts. In fact, the world of unbelievers now is too far out, too distant from the reality of the past. Also, not every believer is equipped with the power to make the blind see as indicated in Ephesians 4:11 (NKJV): "He Himself gave some to be apostles, some prophets, some evangelists, and some pastors and teachers." The body of Christ is not equipped for all the parts to be doing the same things. We were all given the power to perform work according to our calling. We pray for those who are sick, but they might still die. The power of the cross doesn't rely on the believer's ability to perform miracles. Jesus didn't die so we who believe can go around and perform miracles. Rather, Jesus died to reconnect humankind to the kingdom of God. So those who enter the kingdom may find healing themselves and all the other benefits that come with being part of the kingdom of God.

It is certainly important that we show up in the field as Christians to preach and teach. But unlike in the time of Jesus, we are not in business of convincing others to follow Him. This role has been assigned to the Holy spirit of God. Jesus had to perform all the miracles to convince others, and He still wasn't as effective as Peter, Paul, or Stephen in bringing the numbers of new believers to the kingdom of God. Jesus has said it himself. "He that believes on me, the works that I do shall he do also; and greater works than these shall he do; because I go unto my Father." John 14:12 (KJV). Also, He said "But the Comforter, which is the Holy Ghost, whom the Father will send in my name, he shall teach you all things, and bring all things to your remembrance, whatsoever I have said unto you." John 14:26 (KJV). Now that the Holy Spirit is responsible for convincing and teaching all believers, what are our roles as followers of Christ for this new age?

We are to demonstrate the power of the cross in how we live for Jesus. The actions of our faith are our greatest testimony to the effectiveness of the message of the cross. Jesus died so we may show the world a new way of life based on our faith in God. The message of the cross goes beyond this life lived on earth. We must show evidence of a life that goes beyond death. All the disciples of Jesus died, including those who experienced the miracles Jesus and the disciples performed. Our message is to guarantee a success that goes beyond the world that we share to the eternity, which has been promised to all who live not by sight but by faith. Consequently, we are to show a difference in the ways we perform our daily activities. Whether it is business or personal, we also must demonstrate how effective our Christian standards and practices are in terms of producing the success that is promised in the Word we preach. We must hold the truth in every aspect of life, regardless of the domain.

Topical biblical references: Choose your favorite Bible version to check the following references. The NIV is personally recommended.

-Introduction-

Who belongs in the family of God? *(cf. Ephesians 2:11–22; John 1:12–13).*

Those who do not belong in the family of God according to the Bible *(cf. 1 Corinthians 6:9–11; 1 John 3:10).*

Domain 1

Family

The union of a man and a woman to form the society of humankind. The first family was created by God for His glory, which is to be fruitful and multiply. This can also mean to be successful in everything they touch. The two being in perfect agreement is the most powerful spiritual entity know on this planet. The man and woman as a family is the foundation of all societies. The world succeeds and fails on how true the family is to its definition and purpose.

Introduction

In the world, there are many types of family. The basic type, which describes all kinds of families, is what we want to focus on. By that we mean the basic entity formed by a man and woman. Every kind of families starts with this basic formula. Other types of relationships may occur, but a true family needs a man and woman at the core of it to be identified as such. Children are derived from a family. Later in life, the children will marry and have their own families, while the first family becomes grandparents of the new family. Then we have others we adopt as part of a family. Those adopted individuals become part of our family structure, or what we may call the household. Family, however, is related by blood. Other types of families, such as those made of two individuals of the same sex or people with other animal species are not considered in this discussion because they are ungodly and, therefore, not blessed by God.

God, in the beginning, created Adam. A good while after Adam was created, God took Eve out of Adam. Eve was not created a separate being but more of an extension of Adam. The woman certainly has her own soul and spirit. All that is of the flesh, though, she received from the man she is to become one with. The unity of the spirit of the man and the woman is not guaranteed simply because they are made by the same fleshly materials. It is written that what is born of the flesh is flesh, and of the spirit is spirit. The two are not related. Everyone is called to become one in spirit as the family of God. That is not of the flesh but of the spirit. Therefore, we may say there are two types of families. We have the natural type of family, which is made from flesh and blood, and the spirit type, which is the universal family of God. All men and women are called to be part of the family of God, the spirit family, tied together by the blood of Jesus Christ. The natural family is tied together by human blood. Thus, the woman taken out of the man is to become one with the man to make up the family of man, while humankind is to become one with Jesus to make up the family of God.

The family of God is the greatest family of all. Any family of humankind that is not part of the family of God is a lost family. Lost in the sense that there are no divine laws by which that family is governed. If you ought to tell anyone to do and not do anything, there must be a law by which that person is governed. A lost family is not governed by the law of God and, therefore, live by their own laws or without any laws at all.

Everyone needs to be part of a family. No one is to separate from a natural-born family. It is graver danger to be separated from the family of God. This chapter talks about the human family that is the fiber of our society. However, the principles used as guidelines are biblical principles made for the family of God.

This chapter also focuses on the role of the two individuals involved in the human family—the man and the woman—and their roles in making the union between the two works as God intended. Although the focus is centered more on the woman, the role of the man as a husband is clearly defined as the woman seeks to be the perfect wife to her husband. The man is the head of the family, but the entire union and society looks to the woman to keep the moral values and influence greatness in the family of man, and the world society for that matter. For both good and evil sowed as seed in the woman will be widespread. The woman is a key factor in the families of man and God.

Adam and Eve: The Truth Behind the Disobedience of the First Couple toward God

50 The man and the woman have both been placed on earth by God for a divine purpose. That purpose is to walk hand in hand for the glory of God, and it was challenged by a spirit enemy call the devil. The work of the devil is very clear and easily identified. Although the spirit itself does not want to be known, worse being identified, its works can be recognized everywhere. The devil is a lot more influential in places that deny its existence.

God created men and women, placed them together, and declared that no one set apart that which God has put together. Wherever you see things in a different order than what was intended by God, it is clearly the work of evil. The glory for men and women, once they are joined in marriage, is for the two to be in harmony. And those who are married, though there is a lot more glory in their union, will also face the greatest difficulties in life. The force of evil does not wish for the sexes to agree for God has promised that if two agree on anything, He will bring it to pass. And the fact that it is the will of God for humankind to live in peace and harmony is enough for the devil to be against it. For evil goes against all that is godly.

-50-

To identify the works of the devil-Cf. John 8:44; 1 John 3:8; 1 Peter 5:8

Let no man separate what God has joined together-Cf. Matthew 19:6

The Power of Two

51 There is an awesome power in two people agreeing with each other. The power of the man and the woman being together is in the two working together as if of one mind. The Bible says that the man and the woman, after joined together in marriage, become one flesh. It is a great power to be one with another individual. The unity in spirit makes the power of God move better and faster on earth, for it is written, "Again, truly I tell you that if two of you on earth agree about anything they ask for, it will be done for them by my Father in heaven."

The best way for the enemy to gain power over any group is to divide the members. Wherever two or three gather in the name of God, He is there among them, the Bible says. And whenever you see division, the enemy or the devil is present.

Marriage between the man and the woman has always been a challenge for both sexes since creation. It seems like ever since beginning, the woman did not want to listen to the man as she was made to. So why did God put the two together, foreknowing the challenge they had to face as a couple? And the answer is this. It is good. God found that it was good for the man to have a helper. And He created the woman to serve as companion to the first man created, Adam. There is no other plan for the existence of the woman besides being next to her man. Certainly, she can stand alone, for she was also created in the image of God. However, she is most fruitful at the side of her husband to help him live and accomplish the glory of God in both their lives.

Brokenness in the Family of Man: Why Did Eve Eat the Fruit?

-52-

The role of the woman (cf. Genesis 2:18; Titus 2:3–5; 1 Timothy 2:9; 3:11; Colossians 3:19

The role of the Holy Spirit-Cf. John 14:26; Ephesians 4:30

52 God gave Eve to Adam when Adam was still in paradise. The man had everything; nothing was missing. He was the closest to God that any man will ever be. He was well able to care for his wife because he was both spiritually and materially wealthy. And since Eve was the only woman, there was no other woman with whom to compete. It was simply very demanding of Eve to have desired the one thing that was forbidden in the entire garden. And yes, she was tricked by the devil, who told her that the fruit was good to open her eyes. However, Adam had told her what God said about eating the fruit, but she took that bite anyway.

It is the nature of the woman to reach out for greatness. The devil told her the fruit of the tree would open her eyes. That knowledge was appealing to her, who wished good things for her and her husband. How great it would be if something other than disobedience toward God came out of that scenario. Eve would be responsible for opening her husband's eyes and become the greatest figure in the history of humankind.

Women want what is of the highest level for themselves and their families. They possess the vision of greatness. I believe God placed this quality in them to keep men in check, not to fall into laziness and idleness. However, it is not in the authority of woman to make greatness happen for her man. She is more like the Holy Spirit in the life of her husband. The

-53-

Having listened to the woman was Adam's sin, according to the Bible-Cf. *Genesis 3:17; 1 Timothy 2:14*

It is through the woman that sin has entered the world-Cf. *1 Timothy 2:14*

Hebrew word *ezer*, or "help" in English is the same as what the Holy Spirit does in the life of the believer. The woman's job is not to push the issue or take matters into her own hands. Rather, she is to humbly counsel her husband. For although her vision might be great, it is the man God has spoken to as the leader of the family of humankind. The man knows best how to reach the greatness the woman aspires and will achieve it if they both work at it in their own respective places, without competing with one another. The godly position of the wife is simply to remind her husband of that greatness she sees. She becomes dangerous when she assumes the role of a dictator in her family, especially if she is to dictate to her husband what to do.

What Sin Did Adam Commit?

53 We can say whatever we want about Adam. We may even call the very first falling out between God and humankind the curse of Adam. But it is certain that Adam did not receive the first-degree charge of offense for eating that fruit; it was rather like guilt by association. As it is written in the Bible, he received a condemnation for listening to his wife. Based on that biblical fact, let no one tell me to listen to the woman always. It is by the woman that sin entered the world, like apostle Paul said. The man has always been responsible for telling the woman, not the other way around. Equality of the husband and wife in the marriage is not of God's order. The husband is called to sanctify his wife. Again, not the other way around.

A wife who assumes the responsibility over her husband to lead him in the things of God should not have married that man. Also, a wife who will not submit to her husband is leading the entire family toward destruction.

In the current era, husbands have given their wives the leading position simply to keep peace in the family. "She is the boss," many husbands say. And some other men, even pastors, say, "Whatever the woman says." It may not be popular to say this, but biblically, it is of the devil a family led by the woman while the man simply submits to whatever she wants. The enemy wants it like that, so we may be bound to spiritual failure. The man must be the leader of the family. This is the order of God.

Lesson from the Text

- We must not let evil come between us as husband and wife in the way we respond to the challenges we face together as a couple.
- The wife must submit herself first to God and then to her husband so she does not let herself be used as instrument in the hands of the devil to distort her own marriage and the entire family of God.
- The husband must take a firm position on the side of God as the head of the family in order not to be influenced by the weakness of his wife. He must not always listen to his wife but to the voice of God spoken to his conscience and make the right decision, regardless of his wife's personal desires.

- It is not the woman who is in charge of family affairs. The husband is responsible for making final decisions concerning the entire family.
- Although the woman has the ability to stand on her own, her main purpose is to stand by her man so they may together achieve great things for God's kingdom and the benefits of their world society.

Married

54 What does it mean to be married? We know the marital institution comes from God, who put the first couple, Adam and Eve, together for being fruitful and productive on this earth. But what does that mean these days based on what we realize and, sometimes know about firsthand? What does being married mean to you?

Marriage between a man and a woman is not about sex, as the entire world seems to envision. The man's choice of a woman does consider sexual attractiveness, but it should not stop there. Marriage, despite popular fantasy, is 10 percent sexual and 90 percent about caring and being responsible for another person. Yes, marriage can be more work than fun. God is wisdom. He didn't just create wisdom; He is wisdom. He knows that only the great force of universe known as sex could make a man forget how difficult it is to live with another being who is so much the opposite of what he is. However, feminine attraction is so powerful that any normal man would be willing to go against everything he knows and trusts to have that great experience of female companionship. Before he realizes how much a responsibility she really is, a man will do almost anything for the opportunity to simply be with a woman. However, it is not wise for a marital relationship to be based solely on this animal attraction called sex. The wise man will not make his final decision to take a woman for his wife simply based on the fact that she is either great in bed or has an exterior beauty. The intelligent man will look for virtues.

-55-

He or she who desires to be great in the kingdom of God and what they must do (cf. Mark 9:35; Matthew 20:26).

God's command for the husband to love his wife (Ephesians 5:25–33).

Where Is the Sex after a Man and a Woman Are Married?

55 Statically, in most marriage, sex almost disappears completely in time. The sexual attraction between the man and the woman is at its strongest when the two know the least about each other. This is the main reason unfaithfulness is so common. People strive after the unknown, and soon after they reach it, they start to wander off and away from it and to the next new thing, which will become commonplace in time.

There are more important factors in a marital relationship than sex. We have, for instance, mutual agreement, where the husband and wife agree on the same plan to realize great objectives together. This is the main reason women were created. A woman is a vessel of the greatest support to the man.

A woman once told her husband that part of her job as a wife is to complain about things, like appliances that do not work properly in the house. She added that if he didn't want to hear it, he should simply block his ears with two cotton balls. She conceived marriage wrongly. The main concern of the married woman is nothing else but her husband. Her main job is not even the children, if they have any in the marriage. She is to be there to motivate and encourage her husband to greatness. The true wife is one who is devoted to her husband. She is there to pay attention to his needs. Too bad that having the best trained assistants is a privilege reserved to the CEOs of the big corporations. However, a woman who knows her role as a wife will function as the greatest business and personal assistant to her husband. She is positioned to be the key to his success in everything he does.

In reality, today's wife is a separate entity from her husband. Sometimes one does not know what the other is doing. They both are chasing their own dreams and success. They may live together, and even sleep in the same bed, but their lives are not merged. And the passion they once shared as lovers has left without notice. All they have is what they did not plan for at the start of their relationship. All they have is a symbolic marriage.

Marriage is different from friendship or whatever relationship you had before you became husband and wife. Love is also different from romance. The Bible commands the husband to love his wife. This is not a romantic type of love. This is a love that is free of all emotions. This love is an action type of love. This is the love you need to apply when she is not as sexy as she was the first day you met her or when she makes you angry. You need to know how to be patient with her after she's made the same mistake for the seventh time. This is the type of love that God is asking for. The love that will make her be full of passion with you all over again because she realizes you care.

To be a husband is also a great responsibility, especially towards the wife who's at your service. Anyone who uses a tool knows that certain care is necessary to guarantee it functions well. A husband needs to follow certain steps to keep his wife functioning well. The Bible says the wife needs to respect her husband, and the husband needs to love his wife. These are the basic needs for keeping a great relationship between husbands and wives. When these two needs are served properly, a better sense of satisfaction than sex would produce in the husband and wife. In fact, sex is the result in a relationship where love and respect is well served. Love and respect are all a marriage needs to succeed.

At times, it appears more difficult for a husband to please his wife than another man, even a stranger. That's why affairs and unfaithfulness in marriage are so common. The woman finds another man who seems so kind to her, and she becomes involved with him. It's not that the husband hasn't been kind to her. It's simply that he has too much to make up for, while the stranger has a clean slate. The stranger's kindness carries the full effect, while the same act of kindness from the husband goes into paying for something he's done wrong. Most of the husband's efforts to please his wife go into the make-up box. That's why forgiveness is so important in a marriage relationship. One should not have to always be trying to make up for a wrong committed in a relationship years ago.

Keeping score of what the other has done wrong is a great cause for divorce and constant fighting between two individuals who are meant to love and respect each other. God didn't mean for it to be like that. He did not create marriage to be a battlefield.

"It is not good for the man to be alone. I will make a helper suitable for him." Genesis 2:18New International Version (NIV). That's what God said, not that I will make him a sexually attractive and powerful being, impossible to please. Someone he longs after but can never satisfy. I will make him an uncontrollable living nightmare of a companion.

It is of the devil for a woman to make a man's life miserable. The devil has corrupted all that God creates to be a blessing to humankind. The greatest existing pleasure known to any man is a true woman. Although the devil cannot stop the existence of a union between the man and the woman, he will redefine it by placing us in adulterous marriages and defile the God-created institution to something that makes sense to no one.

Men are not so perfect, either. However, it is not a perfect husband that makes a perfect wife. Jesus was the only perfect man who lived, and He was not accepted by His own people in His own land although He was the proven, well-announced Messiah that was to come. The church does not obey to the authority of Jesus as they should, and the Man who is considered the only perfect man is being ignored every day by this church he calls His bride.

One of the greatest dilemmas in life is the lack of respect and honor a man might sometimes experience from his wife. It may be common these days, but it's still one of the most difficult to swallow. Some might say that it's simply the man's ego; but this kind of ego is a sensor placed in the man to let him know that when it happens in a relationship, things are nowhere near normal.

Just like Jesus grieved the church's rebellion against Him, a husband will grieve greatly the lack of respect and honor of his wife. The home should be the kingdom where a husband rules, but not if the husband has a wife who does not honor him as a king. Adultery or infidelity is the only biblical grounds for divorce in a Christian marriage. But a disrespectful wife is lifetime punishment to a husband who intends to keep a dysfunctional marriage.

Lessons from the Text

- ❖ Sex is not the most important factor in the marriage relationship. It is the outcome of a marriage where love and respect are well served.
- ❖ The woman was not created by God to make life impossible for the man. Woman was created to be a blessing to her man.
- ❖ Jesus grieves over the marriage between Him and the church. If Jesus, who is considered the only perfect man who ever lived, suffers in His marriage, a successful marriage does not depend on one partner being perfect.
- ❖ A successful marriage is the result of the woman and the man loving and respecting each other.

- ❖ Men need to stop choosing their women based on external beauty. The woman's best quality is not her behind but her virtues. Both are good, but the latter is what's more important.
- ❖ The wife is not a separate entity from her husband. She's there to help him and not to serve her own agenda.
- ❖ Being a husband is a responsibility. There are steps a husband needs to follow to keep his wife functioning well.

Spirit-Filled Advice about Marriage

Marriage and the three most important issues—sex, fidelity, and loyalty

A man and a woman entering a marital relationship need to at least acknowledge the reality of the three important aspects of that relationship. The first is sex. A man's love for a woman is shown through his need for sex from that woman. If that is kept healthy, the man will be well motivated toward that woman and likely give more attention to that woman. A woman's love for a man is boosted by the fulfillment of her need for attention from that man. Both the man's and the woman's sentiments for each other will fade if their needs are not met.

The other two other factors of a marriage will keep things going if they are not violated. Fidelity in a marriage is defined as both parties belonging to each other exclusively. This needs to be respected on both sides. Loyalty is where many marriages fail or survive and where love and intimacy stand. Loyalty tells both involved, "We have each other no matter what." Loyalty causes both parties to change their plans to benefit each other. If only one shows loyalty to the other, the entire relationship will weaken and fail. Both partners need to be loyal to each other as lovers and as friends. Selfishness kills any relationship.

The Image of Love

56 She may think that because she does not commit adultery with another man she is the ideal wife to her husband, but she might still be disloyal to him. Anyone can be guilty of being disloyal to a spouse by shifting loyalty to an imaginary image of his or her spouse. It may still be your spouse, but it is an image you find attractive. It may not be the person you are married to at all. And many married couples separate because they eventually find the real person in their spouses and are disgusted by it. The character you have in your head that you so much want your spouse to be is what you are in love with. This means you commit adultery in your heart. Everyone may be guilty of that.

A woman is as much of a wife to her husband as she is willing to submit. The husband may be the only person she sleeps with, but her trust, which is her most important asset, she might never place at her husband's disposal. She may never trust him enough to make him the husband that he must be to her. And the less she trusts him, the less intimate they become with each other, meaning the less the two

-56-

God's command for the wife to submit to her husband (cf. 1 Corinthians 11:3; Ephesians 5:22, 24).

God's command for the wife to have great respect for her husband (cf. 1 Peter 3:1–2; Ephesians 5:33).

One cannot please God if not one first believes and trusts Him (cf. Hebrews 11:6).

Without faith it is impossible to please God (cf. Hebrews 11:6)

will become one in any sense. It is written that woman must submit to her husband in all things. Marriage between a man and a woman, as it is intended, only works when the woman is submissive to her husband. Sexual intercourse is overrated simply because it is the only instance when the woman is mostly submissive to a man. Sex may be the only mutual pleasure and connection between a man and a woman.

It is unfortunate that sex isn't the sole factor in the marital relationship. In fact, sex suffers when more important factors, like trust or respect, are lacking. Therefore, you may say the person a woman trusts and has more respect for is the one who will benefit the most from her. The husband might only be someone she uses to serve the person she really values. In short, you may say that no respect means no real marriage—or any relationship, for that matter.

To make matters a bit more comfortable, let's put submission aside and take respect alone as the subject of discussion. Any relationship where one does not have enough respect for the other does not promise any reward. Rather, it will produce tension and heartache for both parties involved. Let's now change the word "submission" to "trust." Most people agree that you must have faith in people. You must have a level of trust in people, so they may be free to perform in any area. Placing pressure on others by not trusting them may not cause them to fail, but it will certainly place you on their scrap list. Without a wife who truly trusts and respects, a husband is better off alone. No one needs this level of negativity from someone as close to you as a spouse, especially one who does not believe in you. Not even God can deal with such level of negativity for it is written that without faith, it is impossible to please God. If your personal core of belief is not supported by your friends, you may need to hang around those who believe in the same things you do. The role of the wife is to support her husband. If a woman finds it impossible to support, trust, and respect her husband by submitting all to him, she is not in a condition to be a wife to that man. That man needs not to consider having a wife. Whatever it is that is not considered useful for a definite purpose is useless to that purpose. Also, a woman who does not trust her husband's judgment enough to confidently submit herself completely to him has no place in that man's life. Trust is a very important factor in any relationship, especially a marriage relationship. And a man whose wife doesn't trust him is dealing with a dysfunctional wife and marriage.

-57-

The husband's responsibility to sanctify his wife, like Jesus does the church (cf. Ephesians 5:25–33).

Sarah as an example of a perfect wife to a not-so-perfect husband (cf. 1 Peter 3:6).

Sarah given to a king by Abraham (cf. Genesis 20:1–18).

How to Fix the Problem of Having a Dysfunctional Wife

57 The Bible says the husband needs to sanctify his wife; that is, to teach her about godly matters. The husband needs to make sure she understands her purpose as a wife and what is expected of her. His role as a husband must be made clear to her also, as well as how he must care for her as Christ cares for the church. This is not personal. It is marriage as God intended to benefit all involved and the society to which the family belongs. A wife not functioning properly, or not playing her respective role as a wife, might have more to do with the husband not doing his job as a husband. He might not be leading her in the right direction or giving her the instructions needed for her to better help him.

A stubborn wife, however, will not be easy to instruct. She's already had her own preconceived idea of what marriage is to her. Most likely, she will not conform to any new order. It matters not that the order comes from God. Her cause and the husband's in that marriage will then be different.

If a wife's primary cause in life is different than her husband's, unless he has nothing on his own agenda to achieve, he needs to stop her from being a primary help to that cause. Otherwise, he will be laboring, involuntarily, for the same cause. Yes, he'll be forced to work for someone else. A large part of his hard work will be applied to support someone or a cause that he particularly would not be involved in. It is nothing if he does not care about how he spends his time and resources. But if he is someone with a dream and a direction for his life, he needs to either have control of his wife's doings or dismiss her from the role of being his life partner, otherwise known as his wife.

A woman's primary duty as a wife is to help accomplish her husband's dream. If her dreams are of greater importance than her husband's and he wishes to join her, they may agree to do so. If they agree on going the same direction, it doesn't matter whose dream they support. But if they have different dreams and directions in life, it is not possible for the two to be together for they won't benefit much from each other. One will constantly be a drag to other.

A woman with a different dream than her husband's will be a hindrance to her husband's destiny and, therefore, cannot fulfill her role as a wife to that man. It is a clear conflict of interest. She needs a husband who shares her dreams and is willing to help and support her. She might have the best plan for her life, but she needs the right man to help with that plan. Marriage is not about who has the best plan, the man or the woman, rather it is about joining and agreeing together to make one plan work. A married couple may also choose to run two separate lives and still be together, but that should be a decision made from the start before they are joined in holy matrimony. If one is depending on the other for help to accomplish anything, that should have also been agreed on from the start. Whichever one needs the help should speak up from the start, otherwise someone will need to hold his or her peace forever. The wife however is the one who is expected and biblically required to submit.

A possible conflict of interest in marriage, presented by the apostle Paul to the church (cf. 1 Corinthians 7:32–35).

A husband needs to make it clear to his wife that he needs to focus on his dream and achieve his objectives in life. Her reaction after that, as a responsible wife, is to help the husband by focusing on making the necessary changes to her routine to help her husband reach his success. If she should continue having a separate list of activities that require him to lose focus on his own efforts to achieve his objectives, he needs to separate himself from that woman and not consider her as a wife until she decides to join and support him in achieving one common dream or purpose for the family. Again, the purpose of a wife is to be a help to her husband. It

-58-

The ideal wife as described in the book of Proverbs (cf. Proverbs 31:10–31).

The story of the two banquets given at the same time by the king and the queen that made Esther royalty (cf. Esther 1:1–19).

doesn't matter what today's society may say. If she becomes more of a responsibility than a help to him, her purpose as a wife is deviated. And so will he be as her husband.

Can a Wife Manage Activities and Projects that Are Not Her Husband's?

58 Certainly yes. A true wife will control the world without disturbing her husband and still have time to be the help she needs to be for her husband. If she is overwhelmed with her own activities and demands her husband's attention to help her, she needs to quit. The same way that you cannot neglect your children to care for your personal needs, a wife is not to neglect her husband to care for the outside activities that are personal to her. If a husband finds no joy in his primary occupation, he needs to change occupations. It is the same for a wife. If she doesn't find joy in being a help to her husband, she needs not to continue to be a wife to him. The wife needs to be devoted to her husband to joyfully fulfill her role as his wife. Her devotion to her husband is key to her joy of being a wife. At some point in every woman's life, she needs to decide whether she will be devoted to her husband. If not, she should find a different role to play and not be a hindrance to that man's God-given destiny. No one should be forced to be a help to another person. All forced labor is known as slavery. Being married to someone should not be forced labor. Marriage is an institution where a man and a woman submit to each other's needs willingly for the personal fulfillment and happiness of both parties.

How about a Husband Making Time for His Wife and Family?

59 Some wives require family time from their husbands to help them with their chores or other personal activities they are involved in. Your role as a wife is not to keep your husband occupied. The man's objectives in life and the many areas of service that God has called him to are enough to do so. A responsible man is a busy man. Family time is off time for a husband. There is no such thing as time for wife. A wife who requires personal time from her husband must be leading a parallel life to him. She is to make herself available to her man, and not the other way around. If she is to occupy herself with other personal issues, and her husband cannot get her attention when needed, he doesn't have a wife.

A husband who loves his wife will know her needs, be they physical or emotional. It is not in a wife's best interest to nag her husband about her needs when he is preoccupied with other responsibilities. That only places pressure on the husband and, in return, causes resentment from him toward her. It is not bad to bring before him some issues that may need immediate attention. But making your husband feel irresponsible does not help your relationship with him. A nagging and demanding wife is a dysfunctional wife. She will blur her husband's focus on important tasks and veer him off his purpose in life. The first woman, Eve, was

-59-

Christ and the church given as an example of a perfect couple (cf. Ephesians 5:25–33).

-60-

The law God gave Moses regarding marriage (cf. Romans 14:17; Luke 13:18–19; Mark 4:26–29; Luke 17:21; Matthew 13:33).

The law of giving and receiving in the Bible (cf. Luke 6:38).

There is far more joy in giving than receiving (Acts 20:35).

a demanding wife. She demanded that her husband, Adam, eat from the forbidden tree. Humankind is still paying for her act of greed and disobedience. To love is not to do whatever one desires. Rather, to love is to care for each other as commanded by the Word of God. To love is not to be supportive of insanity. Sympathy shown to the insane by joining in the insane activities is no help to the insane, and a complete waste of time and energy to the "considered sane". Excessiveness in showing sympathy to others is a dangerous weakness to social wellness and the order of things. Love, nor sympathy are not to be used as excuses to support anyone when that person is clearly out of order.

Lessons from the Text

❖ Being faithful doesn't make a woman a perfect wife to her husband. A woman who trusts and believes in her husband makes the joy of that man.

❖ A wife is not to lead a parallel life to her husband. She should always be on the same team as her husband.

❖ A wife with a different cause from her husband cannot fulfill her duty as a wife.

The Laws of Marriage

60 Marriage. It is the first social institution created by the Creator, God. It is defined as the union between a man and a woman for the advancement of humankind on this planet. Woman was created for that purpose alone. The primary reason for the existence of the female species is for marriage. It is written that it is not good for man to be alone. Therefore, God created a woman, physically taken out of the man to be with him as a help to him. That same woman has become a punishment to men due to a clear misunderstanding between the two individuals and the institution that placed them together as couple. Nor has the man been so much a blessing to the woman in the way it was meant to be. In fact, women have suffered much abuse from the very being who should protect them. To annihilate this fact, men and women need to come to the perfect understanding of what marriage is truly about.

The tremendous force of attraction that join a man and woman is not enough to keep them together, much less make them one as the original plan intended. Thus, they might survive long years together for deep down in their hearts, they know the union is meant to be forever. However, forever in a marriage where the two are not fully satisfied can be a terrible situation for both involved.

Sex is not enough to keep the man and the woman happy in their marriage. In order for marriage to be fruitful or bring great joy for both and those around them, there are principles that need to be taken into consideration. The essential factor in the marriage relationship for both partners is generosity. The greatest problem in any relationship is when one of the parties claims a recipient position, thinking that he or she is there to receive all types of services and not be obliged to give without it being demanded. Can the other party involved in that union help alleviate the issue? Yes, but it takes knowledge and a lot of wisdom to help yourself in a relationship without your personal interest being clearly seen. You must be able to remove yourself from the picture completely and not seeing yourself as having anything to gain. Otherwise, it would be an act of selfishness on your part, and the other person will be very reluctant in taking your advice or counsel. People generally do not contribute to anything that is to profit someone directly unless that person presents them a cause that is in the best interests of many. And in the case of a personal relationship, you cannot ask others to give to you. You can only inspire them to give by your giving. The work must first be done in you. Whatever you feel would be a great benefit to you, bring to the table as a great benefit to others. Just as it is written, "Do unto others as you would like another do unto you." Don't let yourself be seen as the greatest beneficiary in your relationships with others. As it is also written, "The greatest among you will be your servant." If you wish to benefit a lot from others, you have first to place yourself as a servant to their needs.

It is best to have the desire to give and not to want anything from others. The frustration in trying to gain even where you have invested is tremendous. It is almost too much to bear, knowing that you have been giving so much to someone who is not willing to give anything back. And as said earlier, you cannot force anyone to give. Therefore, it is best not to expect anything from others. Yes, even your spouse; especially your spouse. It is a continuous war between husbands and wives, reminding each other of their debts and responsibilities toward each other. If you already have in mind all the benefits you'll receive in a relationship with your spouse, you have already set yourself up for great disappointment. Yes, there is much to benefit from having a wife or a husband, but the entire deal must be clearly introduced that way at the beginning, before the two of you get involved. There must be a clear understanding of what the responsibilities of both partners are from the start. It is too late to claim what neither of you discussed after the ceremony.

It is inevitable for scandals to occur, but cursed be one causing it (Matthew 18:7).

Your being well pleased with evildoers benefits you the same reward with them (cf. James 4:4; Psalm 50:18–21).

The role both partners play in a marriage is stated clearly in the Bible. The best advice before anyone gets involved in this kind of relationship is to know what the one who created marriage says about the institution. Before you start to practice any sport, it is wise to at least know the rules. The same for the great institution of marriage. It is wise for those involved to play by the rules. So we call this the laws of marriage.

A man and a woman joined together in holy matrimony become the foundation of the society of which they are part. In the entire story of Adam and Eve and the forbidden fruit, it is obvious that Eve has broken a rule. She took from the forbidden tree. Adam, however, has broken another rule. First, Eve broke the subordination rule for Adam told her what God said regarding the tree. But Adam broke the leadership rule. He did not have to take a bite. He could have reminded Eve of what God said about eating the fruit from the tree. And if Eve had to be punished for eating that fruit, she would have been the only one to be punished. Adam would have kept his relationship with God, and Eve would probably have to be replaced by another woman. If Adam kept his responsibilities as the leader in this union, the entire world would not have to suffer the consequences of his mistake. Therefore, a man must be careful in his relationship within his marriage to prevent heartaches for the entire society.

Prostitution, for instance, is caused by men being irresponsible leaders for the women involved are daughters and wives of other men. The men involved with a prostitute keep the fire of sin and disobedience burning, which will consume them. No one wins when being irresponsible. We must respect the rules.

The laws of marriage involve the following.

First, we begin with the law that establishes security in the marriage relationship. This law prevents the wife, in her own insecurity, to think she can put an end to the great journey of marriage by separating herself from her husband. The law, as prescribed by the Word of God, says a wife must not separate herself from her husband.

By separate, based on the Vine's Complete Expository Dictionary, it means this *chorizo* (χωρίζω), "to put apart, separate," "to separate oneself, to depart from." The wife must not depart from her husband. It is a common practice for women to simply pick up and go to their parents or friends. A wife does not have the option, though a few women think they can leave and come back when they feel like it, and their husbands are obliged to take them back. Those women do not have the power to make their own rules for the marriage institution. Neither does anyone else, for that matter. The Bible does say in the next verse, "But if she does, she must remain unmarried or else be reconciled to her husband." This is not presented to the woman as an option to leave her husband for the law is that she *must* not leave. But in case she chose to disobey that law, she is presented with the option to remain unmarried or reconcile with her husband. This constitutes the rule of marriage regarding the woman as far as security in the marriage.

The same law toward the husband in relation to time limit and commitment in the marriage is found in the remainder of the same verse. And, it says this: "And a husband must not divorce his wife." The husband does not have the option to divorce his wife.

And so, based on these two rules of marriage for husband and wife, marriage is forever, or until death. God, the Creator of all things and the author of the marriage institution, intended for both man and the woman to feel secure in their relationship and for neither party to assume the other can just take off anytime. For an institution that is considered the foundation of our society, a separation between the two parties would cause great damage to everyone around, including other family members, or worse, the children if any. According to today's statistics, we have plenty of proof of the grave consequences on society caused by marital separation.

Why Divorce in the Mosaic Law?

-61-

Jesus and the law of Moses on divorce (cf. Matthew 19:3–9).

The penalty for violating a woman (Deuteronomy 22:23–29).

Lusting after and sleeping with another's man or woman (cf. Deuteronomy 22:22).

61 It is not a perfect world, and Moses, a great prophet of God, gave men permission to divorce their wives due to the hardness of men's hearts. But as Jesus said concerning this issue of divorce, "In the beginning it was not so." It is not part of God's original plan for men and women to hop from one relationship to another. Nor for a married couple to ever become separated while the two are still alive. As husband and wife, you are to stay together for life.

In case of infidelity, which only applies biblically to the woman, the husband has the rights to take another woman in marriage. The unfaithful wife is considered dead. Under the law of Moses, she would be put to death. There is no law in the Bible where a man is ordered to be killed for a sexual sin except rape or sleeping with another man's wife. "If a man commits adultery with another man's wife—with the wife of his neighbor—both the adulterer and the adulteress are to be put to death."

Polygamy and Monogamy in the Bible

Let marriage be held in honor among all, and let the marriage bed be undefiled, for God will judge the sexually immoral and adulterous

Hebrews 13:4 ESV

62 A man, although married, could take as many women as desired, as long as none of those women was pledge to or married to another man. No place in the Bible does it say a respectable woman could be married to more than one man. It was clearly restricted. The Bible, however, even in Jesus's time, does not forbid men to marry more than one woman, except in a few cases. Yes, a man can biblically take in marriage as many wives as he desires to take, unless that man aspires to be a bishop. In that situation, the man can still take a few sisters in Christ in marriage, but he cannot be a bishop at the same time.

Also, after God delivered the people of Israel from Egypt, He gave a few restrictions for anyone the people of Israel would consider to be king over them. One of those restriction was for the king, "not to acquire many wives for himself, lest his heart turn away, nor shall he acquire for himself excessive silver and gold" (Deuteronomy 17:17 KJV). This was considered more like advice from God than a commandment. But coming from God Himself, this was not to be violated, or some punitive consequences would surely result.

For the rest of the ordinary men who are not called to occupy the office of a bishop or become king, it is not directly indicated anywhere in the Bible that polygamy is wrong, unless one considers it to be in interpreting Malachi 2:15–16. There, God speaks to the people, precisely the husbands, about being faithful to the wives of their youth. It does not mention wives, so one could determine that God intends that a man must have only one wife, to whom he must also be faithful.

-62-

Polygamy is forbidden to men aspiring to become bishops or deacons (cf. 1 Timothy 3:12).

Men having more than one wife in the Bible (cf. Judges 8:30; 2 Chronicles 24:3; 13:21; Genesis 26:34–35; 2 Samuel 5:13; 1 Kings 11:1–8).

Punishment for violating a woman's reputation (cf. Deuteronomy 22:13–21).

One might also want to consider creation for the support of monogamy in the Bible. For God created Adam and Eve, and not Adam and a few women for Adam to pick from. And based on Genesis 2:24 (ESV), "Therefore a man shall leave his father and his mother and hold fast to his wife, and they shall become one flesh," one can say God always intended for a man to have just one wife. However, it is not so clear.

Someone who reads the Bible might ask about this verse: "You have heard that it was said, 'You shall not commit adultery. But I say to you that everyone who looks at a woman with lustful intent has already committed adultery with her in his heart" (Matthew 5:27–28 ESV). Unfortunately, the same Greek word in this passage used to translate the word "lust" is the same one used to also translate the Hebrew word meaning to covet, like we found in the Ten Commandments: "You should not covet your neighbor's wife" or any of his belongings. That word always implies to lust after what belong to someone else. Jesus only reinforced the ancient law found in the Ten Commandments. This is not a new law that forbids any man the desire to take a free woman as his wife. However, that man needs to keep his previous ones, giving them the same love and care as he does the new one. God hates divorce, which is stated very clearly in the Bible.

The apostle Paul wrote in 1 Corinthians 10:23 (ESV), "'All things are lawful,' but not all things are helpful. 'All things are lawful,' but not all things build up." Also, it is written that in the last days, we will be judged for what we have done while living in this flesh. Our main priorities in life is not to defend what is only our own interests. We are also to consider the interests of others. Nowhere in the Bible do we see that those who acquired many wives lived a happier life. And God, if not intended for us to have something or live a certain way, although it is permissible by Him, it is best to avoid, simply due to the fact that it was not predetermined by God to be so. Although throughout the Bible, many have somewhat gotten away with practicing polygamy, monogamy is in the perfect will of God for humankind since creation.

Many laws are found in the Bible that deal with other issues concerning this union between a man and a woman. The following one regards sex in the marriage.

63 The Law of Sexual Purity in Marriage

> Marriage should be honored by all, and the marriage bed kept pure, for God will judge the adulterer and all the sexually immoral. (Hebrews 13:4 ESV)

This law lay down the quality of marriage and the kind of sexual freedom that is permissible is the marriage relationship. Again, the word "adulterer" is mentioned in this passage. It is clear that God is serious about a woman being shared by two or many men who are still alive. Also, sexual immorality and sex outside a godly marriage are both offenses in the Bible. Although men

-64-

Refuse not sex to your spouse (cf. 1 Corinthians 7:3–5; Proverbs 5:18–19).

are given the freedom to take more than one wife, a well-defined boundary is set to the status of women before they become wives. For instance, a godly person is not to marry an unbeliever. The Bible says there is no relation between the two, and common sense tells you that they don't live under the same set of principles. Even in the case of two believers from the same congregation, if they have different views about the teaching of the Bible and other faith issues, it will be difficult for them to have a healthy marriage relationship. If one believes certain things one way and the other an entirely different way, there will always be quarrels and discussions between them on matters of faith, which should be the foundation of the relationship.

It is very important that a man and woman, before they become husband and wife, make sure they understand some key biblical issues the same way. Issues like the complete submission of the woman to the man, for example. Such issues will cause a never-ending war between a married couple if understood differently. It is important to consider all these things to keep a good marriage and the marriage bed pure.

The next law addresses the concern of sexual intimacy.

64 The Law of Positive Response to Sex in Marriage

The husband should give to his wife her conjugal rights, and likewise the wife to her husband. For the wife does not have authority over her own body, but the husband does. Likewise, the husband does not have authority over his own body, but the wife does. Do not deprive one another, except perhaps by agreement for a limited time, that you may devote yourselves to prayer; but then come together again, so that Satan may not tempt you because of your lack of self-control. (1 Corinthians 7:3–5 ESV)

This set of laws favor all men. No husband, except in some very rare and exceptional occasions, will refuse sex to his wife. The wife, on the other hand, may look to find ways to deal with her sexually insatiable husband. The Bible says that she can refuse, with the husband's consent. The husband will consent since it is not the only time he will need to make that same approach. The husband also must understand that his wife needs to be ready, and it is his job to work at it, so they may have a positive response all the time.

65 The Law of Relative Gentleness in Marriage

Likewise, husbands, live with your wives in an understanding way, showing honor to the woman as the weaker vessel, since they are heirs with you of the grace of life, so that your prayers may not be hindered. (1 Peter 3:7 ESV)

God is watching you, husbands, in your relationship with your wives. You need God to be receptive and responsive to you in your prayers, so you need to be careful how you treat your women. For God cares a lot for the women He places in your lives.

If your wife keeps on saying no to you for sex, there might be something wrong with her. It might even be a spiritual problem. Do not get frustrated

-66-

Biblical examples of three great men and husbands being wrongly advised by their wives.

Eve giving the forbidden fruit to Adam (cf. Genesis 3:6).

Sarah advising Abraham to go and sleep with her servant Agar (cf. Genesis 16:1–16).

Job's wife telling him to curse God and die (cf. Job 2:9–10).

with her and start treating her harshly. You get nowhere being upset with your wife about sex. Of course, it is difficult for a man to watch a healthy woman circulating inside the house in all kinds of ways. Then, when night comes, she gets in bed, and as soon as you start making your moves, she turns around and says no. No one does that but a woman.

In any case, God commanded you men to treat women with kindness. Otherwise, He will not listen to your prayers. It is that serious. This is a law you need to be very careful with. For who needs to be ignored by God for fighting with his wife over sex?

Lessons from the Text

- ❖ We need to know what is involved in marriage before we get married, not during or after.
- ❖ For marriage to be the blessing it was created to be, we need to consider and apply the established laws of marriage.
- ❖ God cares very much for the women He put in our lives. We need to treat them as they are considered.

The Man Leading the Woman

66 No man can lead a woman before she has first submitted to his authority with respect. A woman with no good regard toward her husband will not be able to function as a good wife to him. If she feels that he does not have the capacity to be a husband to her that she can honor, she cannot be his wife as described in the Word.

A husband who is not able to provide for the needs of his family does not necessarily have to lose the respect of his wife. However, if because of his incapability the wife chooses to regard him as a nobody, that woman is not fit to be called that man's wife. They might choose to live together until death in a type of marriage, but as for the real definition of marriage, it is not.

The godly wife is she who respects and supports the position of her husband. She may not agree with him but will not stand against her husband. Instead, she will point him in the right direction and never stand against him as his rival.

Even the language spoken by a true wife is different from that spoken by a simple married woman. A true wife, in all circumstances will say, "we," and the woman who considers her man only as a provider says, "you," or, "my husband." For example, the latter would tell her husband, "You don't have enough money. You cannot afford it." Never will she accept the misfortune of her husband as her own. In fact, she will blame her husband for making her part of it. All married women blame their husbands. But a true wife is in it together with her husband and will use her abilities to help him as a team. It's never a question of what she wants but what better serves him as the head and leader of the family. Just like Moses and the people of Israel, if a wife does not approve of the decisions made by her husband, she may cause him to miss his destiny and calling in life. The husband needs not to be frustrated with a

-67-

He who does not care for his own is worse than the unbeliever (cf. 1 Timothy 5:8).

He who loves his wife loves himself (cf. Ephesians 5:28).

The man and his woman together as one (cf. Genesis 2:24).

stubborn wife if he would like to finish his course in the race of his calling from God.

Your wife might be very unhappy and even disrespectful, but as a man of

God, you need to remain focused on keeping your house in order before God to fulfill your calling. The man is responsible to guide and make his woman the product that God created her to be. She might have given you the worst advice in some bad situations. Sarah, Eve, and Job's wife gave their husbands some terrible advice. But she is your wife, and remember that she is a weaker vessel.

Lessons from the Text

❖ True wives do not contest their husbands. Instead, they try to understand the differences between them and their husbands. Then, they try to point their husbands, if able, in the right direction.

❖ A godly man needs not to be frustrated with a stubborn wife if he wants to focus on his calling from God.

❖ A man should have the respect of his wife regardless of whether he can provide for his family.

The Natures of Man and Woman

67 A man created by God stands on his own with God. The woman God gave him to be his wife neither completes him nor adds value to his existence. A man is created in the image of God and has the spirit of his Creator living inside him. That completes man as who he is among all other beings. The woman was taken out of the man by God to help man.

There is a common saying that women are necessary evils. Also, it is said that you cannot live with them, and you cannot live without them. There is nothing evil about anything that God has created. Biblically, a man will do fine without a woman to call his wife. A man with a true wife, however, will do greater things. A woman who is not a true wife to a man will cause him great pain, and at the end, she can destroy him.

Contrary to popular belief, man is a force motivated by love, not sex. The love of God keeps men alive, and His blessings toward us keep us excited. Love is very strongly seen through good deeds. We are to show as many good deeds as we expect to receive to generate love. The greatest enemy of love is not hate but indifference. Not caring for others in the sense of doing good toward them, or simply going through the motions of life, go against the very existence of men. All acts of evil by men toward each other are evidence that the devil is present among them.

Man is a vessel created to be used by God. Once created, God placed His own spirit in them. However, men can also be possessed by the devil. And the devil in a man will make that man hate another man.

A woman is the best representation of men, standing right in front of them. Men love God due to His Spirit in them, and a man loves a woman because she was taken out of him.

-68-

God found it not good for the man to be alone without the woman (cf. Genesis 2:18).

To be betrayed by those who are the closest to you (cf. Psalm 55:12–14).

The wife is to submit to her husband in all things according to the Bible (cf. Ephesians 5:24).

Lessons from the Text

- God doesn't need men to be God. Before men are, God has already been.
- A man can pretty much do without a woman. The man was in existence before the woman.
- The glory of God is seen all over His creations, especially in men. The same is true for men; the glory of men is seen in women. As it is written, he who loves his wife loves himself.

The Nature of a Woman and Wife

A woman is as self-sufficient as fire. Someone needs to start a fire, and it will consume the entire place all by itself. A woman confined in the discipline of the Creator can be used to achieve a great purpose, but left alone to do whatever is the gravest danger to society. She will do more harm than thousands of men put together. All things powerful need a structure and environment to nurture what is good in them for the benefit of that environment.

68 There is a danger in creating something to be the answer to a major problem. The danger is that whatever this creation is, it will have a lot of power in keeping things working. Like a double-edged sword, a woman can be the greatest blessing or the biggest curse. To all that exists, this one rule applies. For something to work it must be consistent to the purpose for which it was created. Women were created for the well-being of humankind. Therefore, a woman becomes the centrepiece, or the key object, to the joy and success of a man.

If any smart being would become the adversary of man and wants to cause real damage to him, the best way is to attack what is most important to him. And that is the woman. It is way more painful to attack what is valuable to someone than it is to attack the person himself or herself. In fact, the major pain of suffering is in the responses of those around that person. My pain is intensified by the inconvenience I see placed upon those I care for and who should care for me. The more sentiment you have for someone, the more that person can hurt you in his or her reaction or attitude toward you.

The relationship between a man and a woman is the mere beginning of life on earth. To Adam, who was the first man created, nothing made any sense until Eve showed up. The woman, to this day, is essential to life. Not only do women bear children for the continuation of humankind, they keep their men happy and motivated to do what God called them to do. If any man is persecuted in his woman, he is truly persecuted. If a man's wife chooses to go a different path than that which the husband has chosen, unless that man leaves that woman alone, he is set to be a very disturbed and confused man.

A woman is meant to be her man's number-one fan. She needs to see him as her leader. Otherwise, she will be the greatest obstacle to her husband's destiny. God requires that the woman submits to her man in all things. This commandment is not one that will ever be accepted very well, especially by members of our current society. But it is vital for the success of a man and woman in a marital relationship. The husband is the head of his wife as Christ is to the church. And God being a God of order will not allow a husband to be led by his wife, nor for her to disrespect her husband in any way.

One flesh is far better than one team. The man is to be made one with his woman to have one vision, not simply to work as a team. Jesus is made one with the church. We, the church, are members of the body of Christ.

A wife who wants to do what she wants for her husband is not a great help to him. She might be the most active person in her husband's life, but if all that she wants to do are things he does not agree with, her business is her own and not that of a wife. The wife is there to support her husband. She is to help the husband achieve his destiny.

The wife was not intended to be the number-one critic of her husband. Nor is she there to tell him what he needs to do. This is how trouble started in the garden, when Eve suddenly took the position to tell Adam what she thought seemed like a great idea. Sarah also had a great idea for helping God accomplish a promise He made to Abraham. Both of those women's ideas still affect our world.

Women are the greatest companions to men, just like men are the greatest exhibits of workmanship in the hands of God. However, the key to being at service to God is for us to submit ourselves to Him. The world today is filled with independent women who want lives apart from their husbands. They are running a race of freedom from men. The same as men striving to be independent from God, women are running away from being under the authority of their husbands. Therefore, the purpose of women at the side of men has long become unmet since they no longer have the desire to submit to the authority of their men.

Lessons from the Text

❖ All things powerful need a structure and a disciplined environment to grow and nurture what is good in them for the benefit of that environment.

The Perfect Woman

69 How do you find yourself the wife that the Bible requires for a man to have? And how is it that women of today are so far from the requirements of God and the purpose for which they were created? What must a husband do to help improve the character and attitude of his wife? And what is the true responsibility of the woman regarding her husband? All of those are questions that a man needs to ask before taking a woman as a wife to guarantee that his marriage has a chance to survive.

No marriage will just simply work because the husband provides everything his wife needs. And some women do not require a man to provide them with anything and still be a good wife. Therefore, what is it exactly that make a woman to willingly

-69-

Women to focus on being beautiful from the inside out, and not so much on the outside, in how they dress, the jewelry they wear, and their hairstyles (cf. 1 Peter 3:3–6).

and happily submit herself to a man regardless of his ability to provide for her? What inspires or makes a woman desire to be a fantastic wife?

Let's have some logic before anything else. How does the relationship between a man and a woman begin in the first place? How does a man lead a woman to be interested in him to begin with? That usually takes a lot of patience and kindness on the man's part toward the woman. For the most part, the man must be very persistent and convincing in his arguments, deeds, and actions to gain the attention and respect of the woman in which he is interested. In short, for a man to get a woman to have the least interest in him takes work. Or did it? The truth is, if you placed yourself from the beginning in position to fight for her love, you will forever have to fight to keep her love.

Many men have wrongly begun their relationships with the women they now have as their wives. One should not need to be flattering or continuously be courting a woman who does not jump at the opportunity to be his wife. She needs to want this, or don't even give her a second thought. The most serious and practical marriage proposal should be an ad in the local newspaper saying, "Help wanted! Responsible man looking for a responsible mate."

A man asked a woman twice to marry him, and both times she said no. There should not have been a second time. Too many women would fall apart for the opportunity to be his wife. He should pick one of them. Instead, he wants to make his life difficult by chasing a woman who is chasing some other man. You are not her type; just leave it at that.

The perfect woman for you is the woman who wants you. Any man who tries to negotiate love from a woman who does not love him is not serious about finding a wife. No wise man needs a challenging woman as a wife. Marriage between a man and a woman was never designed to be that much work. We can eliminate a great percentage of divorces by properly choosing our mates from the start.

Another group of men marry troubled women. She has never complied with his requirements for marriage. She's been disrespectful to him, his friends, and his parents. She doesn't cook. She spends most of her time on the Internet, on Facebook. She has no respect for her parents. You think marriage will fix all that? Certainly not. In fact, it will only make her worse. Marriage does not turn a woman into a wife. A woman can only be prepared to become a wife by her family who raised her, the society where she was raised, and the church she and her family attended when she was still a child. Those who raised her are responsible for the woman she ends up being.

Most parents these days simply believe in the professional training of their daughters. Most of our young women are trained professionals, without any domestic skills. Some have never had any training at all. They were raised to become trouble to the men who end up with them as partners or wives. No one has been a model parent or wife for them to see. Neither their mothers nor their grandmothers were good examples for them to follow. They are blind to the business of having a family of their own. All they know about being a wife is sex. Some are even lousy at that. They think that sex is a way to control their husbands, a method to keep their husbands under their submission.

Some men who are weak fall for it every time; "Whatever you say, honey." Those men don't know their roles as husbands. For them, it's a privilege to have sex 24/7. No one has informed them that once a woman is married, her interest in sex with her husband may diminish. The very reason they took a woman as a wife has become their number-one deception. She is only sexual to men who are nice, to her. And as her husband, you owe her everything. Things you do are less likely to be considered nice because that is your job. Your efforts are taken for granted. Instead of being rewarded, you are more likely to be blamed for not doing enough. You become unpleasant, and since she wasn't too fond of you from the beginning of the relationship, you are now a hindrance to her happiness. You are ready to be placed in the burner. All because neither you nor she were prepared for the business called marriage.

This is how our society prepared our youngsters for marriage. They plan a big party, where parents on both sides get their friends together to join their son and daughter together in marriage. After the ceremony, they close the two youngsters together in a room to consummate their union. That moment is called honeymoon. During that short time, they have sex until their bottoms fall off. They also have a fight or two. Then they have sex again. Then, after that, they fight some more. Then they have sex again. Then the fights between them become more intense, and so does the sex. After a while, the fights become so intense and continuous that they stop having sex. Then they both are having sex with other people. Then they get a divorce.

God created man. Then from the man he made the woman to be a helper to him. As the spirit of God is to the body of Christ, so is the woman to the man. She is to comfort and encourage him. The woman is not a sex object. Therefore, the perfect woman spends more time perfecting her inner beauty and virtues as a wife than her outer beauty. She focuses less on her bed skills and more on moral skills. She works more on her kindness than her boldness. She respects others and tries not to be so straightforward. She is calm and not contentious. The Bible says: "He who finds a wife finds a good thing, and obtains favor from the Lord." Proverbs 18:22 (NKJV)

Lessons from the Text

❖ You don't marry a woman simply because she is physically attractive. A man should marry a woman for her good manners and the way she keeps her Christian values if she attends church.

❖ A man aspiring to become a husband must know he is in the business of raising a family. That includes the wife and children, if blessed with any. He needs to know what he's in for. And he must also have good moral virtues. You cannot give what you do not have.

❖ Great sex does not qualify anyone for marriage. Sex is the result of a great

-70-

Better to dwell in the corner of a housetop than to live with a contentious woman (cf. Proverbs 21:9).

connection between a married couple. A husband without a personal connection with his wife will not have intimacy with her.

❖ The wife is greatly responsible for the good functioning of the family and thus a good marriage. She needs to be of strong character, able to raise the children, and to take care of serious business in the house while the husband goes play with his friends at work.

❖ The man provides everything for his family. That is money, love, and discipline. The wife makes the distributions. She cannot distribute what she hasn't received.

❖ Enjoy the woman you have already chosen as a wife. Work on her character. She'll return the favor. Chances are, no one put a gun to your head to marry her. You know best how to please her.

❖ God hates divorce. He also favors women. She is the last of all that He created and his gift to man. Rejecting a person's gift is the same as rejecting the person. Don't insult God by being unkind to your wife. Seriously, you won't get your prayers answered.

The Contentious Female

70 The purpose of a helper is to make things easier for the person who needs the help. The woman, created for the purpose of being a helper to the man, cannot be contentious. This is different than someone who is simply opinionated. I am referring to a loud, single-minded, violently expressive woman. An unapproachable person of the female species. A contentious woman is a dangerous one. It is written that "Better to dwell in a corner of a housetop than in a house shared with a contentious woman." Proverbs 21:9 New King James Version (NKJV).

The woman helper is made to be approachable. It should be easy to talk to her. She should be so approachable that she is in danger from predators. She should be so nice that her family is afraid she'll be abducted. Just like little children, a woman should be open to all kinds of people, and as a woman, she should be sensitive to the needs of others. These traits are to be to all women, not some particular type.

The woman is made to occupy vital positions in our society. She is to welcome others and make them feel at ease. She is to teach our children. The woman is to neutralize all tensions her man experiences in facing all the issues of life and livelihood. Some women—too few of them—are positioned to function as such. Most are preoccupied with their own needs. Many women position themselves to be served and taken care of. Many give the impression that their greatest service to humankind is to have been born with a vagina. The fact that a person was born a gender does not contribute anything other than the number of a particular gender in that society. Being born a man or woman does not limit you to simply being part of a sex group. One must also function within the responsibilities corresponding to the gender he or she was born with. The man as well as the woman must stand in character and operate in

-70B-

Do not argue about opinions (cf. Romans 14:1; 2 Timothy 2:14).

the role he or she was created to serve. Don't just be a male or a female. Be the man or the woman you were created to be.

The contentious female is a curse. Anything that does not function in its normalcy falls under the category of things that are cursed. Humankind in general has been cursed with abnormalities, and the contentious female is one. A spiritual door has been left open, and the devil was able to enter a woman's life to cause her to be contentious. It may have been the door of unforgiveness. All sins are certainly interrelated with the original sin committed in the garden by Adam and Eve. However, some people open doors to all kinds of new demons in their lives.

Jesus paid the price for all sin at the cross. That sacrifice, which is physical and spiritual, relieved humankind of the original consequences of sin. We do not need to operate under the penalties or the old consequences of the original curse. We can renew our spiritual minds to be the people God intended us to be. A contentious female does not have to be. It is a foolish spiritual choice for a woman not to develop herself to the woman of God she was designed to be. She simply does not accept the divine option to be a complete woman, able to function in the society of humankind. Even if she attends church, a contentious female, if not renewed and transformed, cannot properly be used by God to function within the family of humankind or of God.

The spirit that drives the contentious female functions in the negative. It is not of the order of God and, therefore, does not have good intentions.

That spirit does not promote peace. One cannot trust that any contentious female will reason for the sake of the truth. Her objective in any argument focuses on finding faults. It can never be her fault for she does not take responsibility for anything that is wrong. She has a terrible fear of guilt. Her unreasonableness makes all close and long-term relationships difficult or impossible.

A. How do you help such a character to be better?

You cannot make peace with such a character. She makes peace with you when you finally decide never to respond to her arguments. Not that you must agree with everything a contentious female says. Simply, there's no need to argue since it will only make matters worse. This truth is applied in the any relationship but more specifically with a contentious female. As long as it is up to you, seek peace with everyone. And since everything wrong is your fault anyway, don't feel that you need to reprove her for any wrongdoing. Such women do not take reproofs very well. It will simply come out as a serious accusation. Then the focus will turn on you and everything you have done wrong.

The best way to bring positive change to other individuals is to teach them by being the best example. You simply must practice what you preach right in front of them. It is a difficult task to make disciples because it involves living your own message to simply pass it on. It is then you will be able to make the difference that God desires for you to make in the lives of those around you, and the world.

B. How bad a character is a contentious female?

We are all guilty of some sort of an abnormalities, whether spiritual or physical. Every day we wake up, we are slowly dying. We have all kind of bad habits that we constantly try to break. So we don't think of anyone being in a worse place than we are. We can only be happy that we have found solutions to some of our problems. We are all exposed to the same risk of the same abnormalities. Our real strength is found in helping others find their strengths. We are not to glory in others' defeats, not even our worse enemies. We are to defend the truth in how we show it in our lives. If we are so much against what others do that is wrong, we must not do the same. In all, we must love each other. To be contentious, whether be a man or a woman is a very aggressive mindset. Whatever the reasons that cause an individual to end up in that kind of spirit could not have been a great experience. A contentious person is also a victim from that individual's own attitude. It is a difficult life not to be able to get along well with other individuals. So therefore, one is to be patient with a contentious person. We are required by God to love everyone without exception. Love is the solution to the majority of problems one individual encounters with another.

Lessons from the Text

- We are not to contest the contentious female. We will only aggravate the situation.
- Do not take pride in ourselves based on faults we find in others. We are not better simply

because we don't share certain abnormalities. Instead, we are better because we can model the strengths they need to prevail.

- No one is exempt from their responsibilities to love another based on that person's imperfections. We are to love everyone, especially those with imperfections. They might need it most. We can all relate to this fact.

Submission

Submission is a sign that a person serving as a subordinate is willing to cooperate so the entire team succeeds in a plan that was set for success.

71 In all that God has established and done, He first created a system of operation to help bring about the result He has intended. In all systems of operation, there is a head to lead and communicate with the rest all that is necessary to have the flow of productivity needed to achieve the goal. For example, in the heavenly system of operation, there is a godhead that is Jehovah Himself. Then you have Jesus, who is submitted to God, and the Holy Spirit, who submits to Jesus and to Jehovah God. In the earth realm, God established the church as the system of operation before the people asked for a king to lead them. Before the church, there were the prophets to communicate God's message to the people. As it is written, God first established the prophets and then the rest. What is the purpose of a leader, and what is

-71-

All are in subjection under Christ who is in subjection under the Father-Cf. 1 Corinthians 15:27-28

The biblical order in the service of the church-Cf. 1 Corinthians 12:28; Ephesians 4:11-12

The command from God for all to submit to governing authorities-Cf. Romans 13:1-7

Rather to obey God than man-Cf. Acts 5:27-29

-71A-

To be submissive to one another- Cf. *Ephesians 5:21*

God holds the power to place and discharge all authority- Cf. *Daniel 4:17; Psalm 62:11; Proverbs 8:15-16; 1 Samuel 15:22-23*

the true function of a leader? And why is it necessary that we submit to leaders and all established authorities as required in the Word of God? What kind of importance does God place on leaders and authorities?

It is written that all authorities come from God. And God who has established the authorities demands certain privileges and protection for them. Once a certain individual is anointed as king or called to ministry as a prophet or pastor, it is required by God that you submit to the person's authority and that you must not touch God's anointed as to harm them. The same for all the leaders God has established to guide them His people. You simply cannot touch God's anointed, and we must respect all established authorities.

When it comes to the family, the fabric of our society, God established the husband as head and leader over it to guarantee the well-functioning of this very important part of our world and social system. The family is the foundation of all society. And before all the earthly authorities were, the husband was the sole representative of God on earth. The husband is truly the first earthly authority established by God.

A. Why is it important to submit to the established authorities, including a wife to her husband?

Liability. It is an awesome privilege to be a leader, but it is also a load of pressure to be responsible for an entire operation when others are involved and contributing their efforts. People can be very negative and controversial. There is a comfort in seeing things from a different perspective when you are not responsible for the entire outcome. Many have a better shot at the goal when they are completely off field. Put them in the same position, and it's an entirely different ball game. Based on that, it is important to let the leader lead. The best way to help is not to interfere. Instead, ask how you can help the leader. It is not your place to dictate from the outside what you think is best. Wait for the leader to ask you. You may kindly give advice, but don't feel bad if it's not considered. Be part of the team in your position. Your turn will come when you must lead, and you will appreciate the chance to make the important decisions that guarantee success in your endeavors. Meanwhile, be the best help to whoever needs it.

It does not make anyone smaller to take orders. Those who give orders simply serve them. All orders come from commanding situations. It may seem that someone is passing on those orders, but, they are not. They are receivers of the same orders they give. They have no choice but to give them. If per chance the orders given don't seem right, execute the orders before you come with your suggestions. And don't forget that suggestions are not new orders unless they have been considered by the person responsible to call them such.

There is a special blessing on those positioned to lead others. They may be wicked, but remember that God leads all leaders. He will not let a leader mislead his chosen people before He takes away his leadership. The person really responsible is God, who has power over all situations and leaders. If God is your leader, there is no need to fear anyone will lead you the wrong way.

> "Wives, submit to your own husbands, as to the Lord. For the husband is head of the wife, as also Christ is head of the church; and He is the Savior of the body. Therefore, just as the church is subject to Christ, so let the wives be to their own husbands in everything." (Ephesians 5:22)

This may be the most controversial verse of the Bible. It is also the single answer to a lot of trouble encountered in humankind's family and our society. Followed correctly, people would know how to live better together, as a real family was intended to be.

Nothing works without first being in order. And the marriage between a man and a woman cannot work properly unless we are willing to submit under the authority of God, who created the marriage institution, and do things His way.

The greatest form of submission known to humankind is that which exists in the marital relationship between a man and a woman. However, submission did not start with the woman. Nor does it ends with her. It is a principle of life for one to submit to another for things to function well. Everyone must learn how to properly submit to another. Then we will all know real success and harmony.

B. How must a woman submit to her man?

The exact way prescribed in the Bible. God would never ask us to do something unless there was a reason for it. And the only way for us to benefit from the plan of God is to follow His instructions as given. We are not obeying men by doing what God says regarding men. If God asks us to do anything that seems to lower our security level before our enemy, remember that it is God who is guarding us. Our security is in His hands. It's not like we are putting ourselves in danger. We are obeying the Word of God, who guarantees us that not one hair will fall off our heads without His permission.

So, therefore, woman, put your faith in action, and do as your Father God tells you to do. You will receive all the blessings there are by obeying this piece of scripture. Forget your ego. Remember what Jesus said about anyone who wants to become His disciple; you must renounce yourself. It is not about you but about God, who knows best how to win all fights against the enemy and how to succeed in all that you touch, including your marriage.

C. How must a woman respond to her husband's need for her to submit to him?

God intended the man to grow in all areas, and nothing can help make the man reach his highest level of success than having the "perfect" woman in his life. A woman set out to understand that man's position every moment of his life and willing to support him in those moments. A woman to serve both as that man's cheerleader and adviser. Many men will be successful, but all need a family and real people to truly enjoy their lives. The greatest pain to humankind is solitude. It is not good for man to be alone. The proverbial saying, "Success is nothing

-71C-

Marriage compared with the relationship between Jesus and the church (cf. Ephesians 5:25–33).

without someone with whom to share it," is true. And the greatest form of misery is not having nothing; rather, it is having no one. Real growth requires real people and real challenges.

The greatest challenge is found in the marital relationship. Two individuals join to procreate life and continue God's legacy of humanity in the basic form of a family. For that to happen, there needs to be a game plan, and all parties involved need to understand that what they are part of is greater than they are. Everyone needs to submit to each other at different moments in time. The woman, who is the most valuable player of the entire institution, needs to willingly submit herself under the leadership of a man. The man has no idea how much trouble he can cause, leading his family in the wrong direction. However, if all are willing to submit themselves to the One who created the team, the sport, and the field, though they will stumble some, they will succeed.

"Submission" is a very controversial word, mostly because people place great value in their free will. No one easily submits to the authority of someone else. Not even children want to submit to their parents.

The most common form of submission between the man and the woman happens during sex. The man expects his wife to submit to him during intercourse. In other words, to be in complete agreement that he is the one mainly responsible for the success of this great moment. Her wanting him to be dominant in that moment proves her full cooperation. Without her cooperation, every effort on the man's part is a complete waste of precious energy. The woman's cooperation, or submission, makes the moment a pleasant one.

No matter how pleasurable sex can be, the greatest form of submission a man can ever enjoy from a woman is one most will never know. That is spiritual submission. To explain that, we must first acknowledge that a woman is the most complex spirit being. Any husband who can satisfy his wife's spirituality will know the greatest joy from a woman.

God, who created man and woman and established the institution of marriage, also provided regulations for both partners to follow for that relationship to work well. Whether the husband finds corporation from his wife or not, it is the husband's duty to lead his wife in matters of spiritual importance. A man without any spiritual knowledge, who does not understand the basics of his spirituality, should not place himself in position to lead a family. Such a man will fail to follow established biblical guidelines that are there to make the union a successful one. Although members of an entire family may choose to follow their own distinctive ways, it is the responsibility of the man, as head of his family, to present all the members with the biblical principles for them to follow. His job as a husband requires a lot of patience and faith, and for him to have a great relationship with God through prayer.

No one wants to submit to foolishness, especially a woman unless she is mad. Most men are attracted to mad women because these men seek to take advantage of women in their weakest moment in life, and at the end, have created more madness for those women to deal with. Madness is what those men seem able to contribute to a woman's life. But once a woman comes to her senses, she will not want to submit to no one's madness anymore and will look for someone more productive to be part of her life. Or she might stay in the relationship for reasons I don't know, but women do such things. However, she will find a connection to someone with whom she can share issues that are most valuable to her. The husband, on the other hand, might enjoy her physically, but the person who controls her mind has a lot more power over her than the husband. It is a terrible situation for a husband not to share his wife's spiritual values, or vice versa. The person who shares her spiritual values and with whom she connects on that level has a great influence over the entire family.

D. Vowed to disagree.

The greatest difficulty a man and woman may encounter in a marriage is constant disagreement. It is not a virtue for a woman to have many strong opinions. A man who is serious about having a great family will stay away from such a woman. She may not have a clue about how to do something, but will surely give instructions on how you are to do everything. Such a woman also has a dramatic character. There is no middle ground with her. She either gets her way and is happy, or no one will have peace. The Bible identifies such a woman as being contentious. A contentious woman is not attractive, but men marry them for reasons I don't understand.

A strong and godly woman submits to her husband. If she has any doubt that he doesn't know what's he's doing, she turns to God to guide them both. She will not dismiss her husband of his authority and take charge for she knows that she will only make matters worse. Everything was created in a specific order. No wise person wants to be the one responsible for breaking that order. As it is written. "Jesus said to his disciples: 'Things that cause people to stumble are bound to come, but woe to anyone through whom they come.'"

Do not resist authorities, whether your husband or the law. Instead, pray for them. God is in control, and He is also able to change hearts. Take your complaints to God if you're being ignored by the authorities. He has the power to make all crooked lines straight. As it is written: (I will go before you and make the crooked places straight; I will break in pieces the gates of bronze and cut the bars of iron.) Isaiah 45:2 (NKJV)

Lessons from the Text

- ❖ All authorities are established by God, and we need to respect them as commanded by Him.
- ❖ Let the leaders lead and make the final decisions; they are anointed for such tasks.
- ❖ God will not let His children be led by fools for long. He can change leaders' hearts or remove them from their places of authority.
- ❖ You can be of great service to someone if only you are willing to submit.

❖ Taking orders doesn't make anyone inferior. Those in the position to pass the orders only serve them as commanded by the situation they are in.

❖ When you submit to someone, you obey God, not the person to whom you submit.

❖ Fools do not take complete advantage of their own leadership positions, like a husband who does not have any influence over his wife's spirituality. He who has the wisdom has the real power.

Spirit-Filled Advice about Family and Marriage

Marriage is the union between two beings who are both the same and completely the opposite of each other. However difficult it may seem for the two to get along, due to the constant disagreement fueled by evil sources, it is still a perfect union made by God to accomplish great things on this planet. Much power is vested in the family of humankind, and with that power comes great responsibility. Both the man and the woman are responsible for keeping the family of humankind a success, thus humankind society and the planet. It all depends on the two working together as God intended for the world to be a great place to live. The major problems we have in our society all come from the failure of the family structure. Anyone serious about fixing the world will start with the family. Anyone serious about the destruction of the world and humans will also start with the family of humankind. The devil knows that well.

The first family recorded in the history of humankind was a dysfunctional one. First, the woman, Eve, was tempted with evil. Then evil continued in the children; Cain murdered Abel. That proves the devil's intention for humankind and his ability to destroy us. However, we still hold power over the devil, and that power is nothing but obedience to the Word of God. The plan for humankind's happiness on earth was laid down by the Creator since the beginning. The only problem is that we have refused to trust God. All we need for the greatest experience we have ever had as a family is obedience, not to the devil, but to God's Word.

He who is faithful in the little will be faithful in much-Cf. Luke 16:10; Luke 12:42-44

The wealth of the wicked is destined to go to the just-Cf. Proverbs 13:22

Domain 2

Success

Success is reaching by the means of legitimate efforts a predetermined goal. Get done what you set out to do. Success can also mean to be content; to be in the zone where you are satisfied with who you are or what you've become. To have peace. Everyone is looking to be successful, but only some have a clear understanding of what real success is.

Real Success Is a Divine Matter

72 Many are the ways of wrongdoings, yet there is usually only one right way of achieving something great. Many ways to failure, but one way to achieve real success. You may experience what you might have thought would be the greatest life and end up being miserable. Whatever life you may be living, if it doesn't describe what God in the Bible calls life, you are not experiencing good living. Life is not waking up every day to the works that you either have started or are still trying to accomplish. Rather, life is living the dream God placed in your heart. You will not be happy doing whatever. You will only be making a living doing something that makes you money. However, the real joy of living comes from working in the area and environment where you use your God-given gifts to serve others.

Success is not achieved at the end. Rather, it starts from making the right decision at the beginning and then going through a process until you finally achieve what you have rightly decided at the beginning. If the initial decision is wrong, it doesn't matter what the ending is. It's like the wisdom of Thomas Merton about people climbing the ladder of success only to find out at the end that the ladder was leaning against the wrong wall. That is devastating. The days of our lives are numbered. We do not have an eternity to enjoy life. Living a miserable life, wasting years doing foolishness while we could be seeking what God wants us to do is hilarious. There are no rewards in heaven for doing just something. No matter how great that something might be. The only rewards are for doing what you were intended and equipped to do. We are not here to impress anyone. We are here to serve by using our talents, and others will simply be impressed. Real success is divine. Find it by first seeking God.

-73-

Remember that a good reputation is worth more than great riches-
Cf. Proverbs 22:

Money is not to horde up and be kept for yourself-Cf. 1 Timothy 6:17-19

The Jesus parable of the unfaithful servant-Cf. Matthew 25:14-30

The judgement of God in the last days concerning your businesses on earth-Cf. 2 Corinthians 5:10; Revelation 22:12; 1 Corinthians 4:5

Stewardship v. Proprietorship

73 Your life is not yours but God's. You did nothing to bring yourself in this world, and there is nothing you can do to keep from taking the exit out of this world.

Everyone has the responsibility God gives them toward certain aspects and issues in life. The fulfillment of your God-given responsibility will qualify you for your personal rewards from God in the living world and in the afterlife. Those who take life personally and make it their business to own their positions instead of serving in them will never experience the full benefit of that position. The same for those who are possessive of material things. They often suffer from anxiety and fear of losing what they usually sacrifice so much to achieve. Therefore, knowing that it is not yours but God's, given to use and serve others, places you in a better perspective to enjoy life. He who placed you in this position can find you other and better positions in which to serve.

Absolutely everything anyone might possess belongs to God. You came with nothing, and you will leave with nothing. You are only here to do your service, using whatever privilege you may have. It is in no one's best interest to act like he or she will always be in the same position. You will not live forever. And worse, you may become incapacitated or dismissed from your current position. The only thing that will remain is the legacy you leave behind based on your character. People remember character. Therefore, one is better off having the best of character. For you may not own your position, but you own your actions in that position. That is exactly what God will hold you accountable for.

Spirit-Filled Advice about Stewardship

Stewardship is simply the act of taking care of what belongs to someone else or that which you are using for a specific purpose. People simply take life for granted, as if it were theirs to spend however they wish. Although it was given to you to enjoy, loads of consequences come as the result of someone misusing or abusing this one-time privilege called life. Many find themselves miserable from doing what they thought was pleasing for a moment. It is not against nature for anyone to seek whatever it pleasurable. However, pleasure is found by first pleasing God, who gave this life to you in the first place. It was never your idea to wake up one day and start breathing, and to grow and become. There must have been a purpose behind this major production called creation.

Before one starts using a new piece of equipment, it is wise to know what it was made for and how it functions. Most jump at life as if they lived a thousand years before this life and know all about it. Some smoke, yet no one is born with an exhaust pipe or a chimney stack to his or her side. They have no clue, but they are doing it anyway. In truth, God created you for His glory. You are the best piece of equipment He has ever made. Learn why you were made, and you will be able to make better use of yourself and the short moment you are here to live.

How Much of Our Efforts Really Contribute to Our Success?

-74-

As a man thinks in his mind, so he is, the Bible declares (cf. Proverbs 23:7).

Acquire knowledge, with all you got, get understanding- Cf. Proverbs 4:7

A reading recommendation - Reference to another great book to read As A Man Thinketh - by James Allen

74 It is biblical that as a person thinks, so he or she is. However, things are not always the way we expect them to be because we are very limited in our thinking. A thought and an expectation are not the same. Thoughts are products of your beliefs, which produce the expectations that match those thoughts. These expectations come after the thoughts and are as stable as the thoughts that produce them. You will not achieve anything greater than what you can conceive in your mind. Those who think big will achieve big. And those who think small will achieve small.

Faith is our greatest key to success. One needs to believe in his or her heart and then achievement will be possible. The greatest personal contribution to your success is the knowledge that brought you the motivation to achieve. One must be confident to achieve greatness. Many have the academic background and the education but lack the spiritual foundation to reach desired altitude. It is a negative world out there. You need a great positive force to stand against the opposition. Otherwise, you will carry the greatest power but have no drive. There is no greater advantage than the knowledge that produces faith. The Bible declares: (So then faith comes by hearing, and hearing by the word of God.) Romans 10:17 (NKJV). Your contribution is to acquire the knowledge of the Word of God to produce the required level of faith to achieve your destiny. Wisdom is the greatest way to achieve success. All other knowledge you can buy. Wisdom, however, comes with seeking God.

Spirit-Filled Advice about Your Efforts

Success is not in the amount of effort someone puts into achieving tasks but, rather, in making specific efforts that contribute to a clear vision. It is in making the right choices for your cause. Success is in the staying on course with your dream or vision. Before making any move, one needs to have a clear vision in the heart of what it is that was said or seen. Have you had a word from God? Did God give you a vision, or you are simply doing things? No one is purposed to just wake up every morning and start moving. It best to know why we are moving and toward what direction. We are all created for a specific purpose, and you need to find it, or all your efforts will amount to nothing at all.

Success as God Gives It

75 The road to success is like alcohol. Many get drunk on the way with the idea of going somewhere great and fulfilling, but to everyone's dismay, the destination never seems to be worth the journey. Once they become sober and completely disappointed, they again take the same journey, hoping to reach a better destination. Success, in the sense of instant gratification, is just for a season and is not to be chased. Wisdom, which is the guaranteed way to real success, must be

-75-

To seek wisdom as you do money (cf. Ecclesiastes 7:12).

All that a person can do is made possible and empowered by God (Ecclesiastes 5:19–20).

Do all for the glory of God (cf. Colossians 3:23; 1 Corinthians 10:31; Proverbs 16:3).

the object of life's search. It is one thing to achieve something, but it is another thing to experience complete satisfaction. No achievement, great or small, is guaranteed to bring complete satisfaction to the one who achieved it. However, one who has achieved knowledge and understanding does not need to accomplish greater deeds to be completely satisfied. Contentment and complete satisfaction come from having the knowledge of God, who equips all humankind for great achievement for this glory. Without giving glory to God, all great achievement, although it will benefit many, brings no lasting peace to the one who achieved it. It is a grave sin to steal glory from God, who gives us the ability to achieve. It can even be deadly as reported in Acts 12:21-23. (NIV)

Everything has been given to humankind, and there is nothing we have that we have not received. However, for our participation in the completion of God's creations, we claim more credit than the Creator who makes us able. Without God to inspire the human race, no one will be able to even think of anything good to accomplish. All things are possible to those who believe.

The greatest accomplishment for humankind to realize is that which they have lost since creation. Nothing will better impress God than someone who glorifies Him for who He is and what He has done. This is where we have failed, and it is certainly where we must pick up again. Anything besides acknowledging the power and following the will of God contributes nothing to the essence of humankind and, therefore, brings no real satisfaction. People have achieved great things and made themselves a lot of money and yet never experience real joy and personal satisfaction. Many have realized their biggest dreams and have not known happiness and joy. It is no big deal unless there is a word from God behind it. If God has not promised it, no matter how great a promise, it is an empty one.

Masters of Attention

76 There is a lot we can do to glorify God. The one downfall of it all, however, is that sometimes we might find ourselves in the middle of it and miss the opportunity to give God all the glory in what we are doing. There is a fine line between performing for the glory of God and performing for our own glory. It is human nature to call on the world's attention and say, "Look at me, world. Look at what I can do." In all that everyone can do that is good, God will find glory in it for it is He who gives the ability for all to do whatever they may be able to do. All good things come from God. And whether we give Him the glory for what we can do, He is still the author of all good deeds on earth or heaven.

Most of us think way too highly of ourselves and take the grace of God too personally. Everyone needs to check on their levels of humility to recognize whether they are doing too much to be seen by others. It is natural for people to be boastful about themselves. There are world industries dedicated to the support of showing off blessings they do not possess. Every day, people use every chance they get to present to the world a level of success that they

-76-

Don't boast about yourself (cf. Proverbs 27:1–2).

Don't think too highly of yourself (cf. Romans 12:3).

It is God who is to set a table for you in front of your enemies (cf. Psalm 23; Psalm 81:10–12).

Get over yourself (cf. Proverbs 12:15; 24:6; 15:22; 19:20).

-77-

An old prophet eaten by a lion (cf. 1 Kings 13:15–32).

haven't yet reached. And since all their efforts go into telling lies, they now must try very hard to cover up the fact that they haven't been as successful as they appear to be. So they may have to go deeper into debt to remain in the positions they are assumed to be. If only they would accept their true positions in life and make personal commitments to gradually grow to where they would like to be, many would not have to struggle so much in life.

The most commonly repeated mistakes are caused by refusing to get over ourselves. If one is not prone to change his or her character to fit one's calling, the individual is bound to repeat failures. You are not to focus on yourself as if you were the author of your success. Rather, see yourself as a great example of the grace of God and a source of blessing to others, enemies included.

Those who consider themselves your enemies will certainly see you succeed. God made a provision for you, who some say will not reach your potential or accomplish your dream. But it is not for you to make sure that they see you in the middle of your success. It is God's place to set the table for you in front of your enemies. Your place is to make them feel comfortable at your table and be a blessing to them.

The Promises of God to You and the Courage of Others around You

77 The promise of God from others' perspectives, even from those who are concerned, will not lead you to your destiny. No one can better feel or have a better understanding of what God has promised you than you. When it is unclear how it will happen, it may not be the time to open your heart to the advice of those waiting with you. Not everyone's level of patience is the same, and everyone has a limit to how much suffering they can endure. Your promise from God does not rely on anyone else's courage. It relies only on your own measure, which God has given you. You are not to rely on others' strength to see the fulfillment of God's promise in your life. Nor is one's weakness to be blamed for not reaching your destiny. When everyone might think that you have suffered enough and that it is time for you to do something, if God does not place it in your heart to do so, don't do it.

Great prophets have lived the consequences of others telling them when it is time and what they must do in situations where the Word from God is different from what seems logical. Adam, Abraham, and Moses are a few examples of great servants of God who listened to other voices beside His. They all knew well what God asked them to do, but each listened to those around them who had different perspectives of what was said. It shouldn't have mattered how others saw the situation. They should have done what God told them to do. Instead, they failed under the pressure of their surroundings.

I have the promise of God to be very blessed if I do something exactly the way He asked me to do it. I have other promises that are small compared to a greater vision. The smaller promises are temporary reliefs before I reach the greater one, which is my destiny. It is not easy to perceive how any of the promises of God, great or small, will come to pass. However, God is faithful.

Don't let anyone lead you the wrong way to what God has promised you simply because time is difficult, and they don't see how your dream will come to reality. God is the One who has talked to you; fix your hope on Him. Although times seem hard and people around you are falling apart, know that God is faithful, and you will surely see the Promised Land.

Spirit-Filled Advice about Due Season

People want the best for their loved ones, however, God knows what is best for all and when it will come to pass. The amount of pressure one may receive from those who are concerned can be the cause of failure. Jesus told one of the disciples that His time had not yet come. And when one of the disciple tried to stop Him from taking the cross, Jesus rebuked him, saying, "Get away from me, Satan." It is not always in your best interests what others want for you, regardless of how much they care. God knows what and when. It is you who must stay connected to God so you have a clear signal from the Almighty when and how to make your move. Don't lean on your or others' understanding to tell you what God wants you to do. This concern is only between you and God.

Success Preached to a Lost World

78 Preaching material success to this generation is like selling land to the people in the time of Noah, right before the deluge. The only real success for humankind since the fall of Adam and Eve is for us to be reconnected with God. We had everything before then, and after the fall, everything fell apart. Now that we are given a chance through Jesus to be reconciled with the Father, there is no message more valuable to preach, no knowledge greater than the gospel of Jesus.

The gospel of Jesus goes as such. God, the Creator of the universe, reconciled humankind with Him through the blood sacrifice of His Son, Jesus Christ, so that we may once again be under His full protection and complete provision. We preachers are not to place the carriage before the horses and preach the message of the blessings of God without getting people to reconnect with Him. The truth is we are all under God's protection. However, we often fall from His protection when we violate His commands for living. God cannot protect us if we voluntarily cross over into enemy territory. There is a definite purpose why there are certain things that God tells us not to do. And a purpose why we are required to act certain ways in certain situations. God doesn't make rules just to make rules.

When we sin against God, we violate the law of His nature. That automatically places us under the authority of evil to do with us as he pleases. God's forgiveness of our sins, when we ask for it, makes use of the blood sacrifice of Jesus that paid for our sins

There is no more sacrifice for someone who sins voluntarily (cf. Hebrews 10:26).

Business as usual while a breeze of sudden destruction is coming over (cf. 1 Thessalonians 5:3; Matthew 24:38).

Do not give way to the devil (cf. Ephesians 4:27).

and places us back under His protection. By placing more focus on material things than we on spiritual things, we tend to bypass the supremacy of God and give glory to His blessings more than we do Him. Although the blessings of God are what we seem to need to operate on this planet, they cannot provide us with the full satisfaction that only the presence of God can give. One may have gotten a lot of money for products or services provided to others, but if no one has anything to offer in return, all the money collected will be of no use. What will you get in exchange for all the money you worked for when everyone is barren, unproductive? Or, say you have all the money, but anything of any real value that's for sale is for members only. That is the same for the kingdom of God. No money in the world can provide you with real blessings that God put aside for those who are in a relationship with Him.

Some things are reserved for club members only. And the kingdom of God, or heaven, is the greatest club there is, with blessings that are reserved for its exclusive members. Your best bet is to make yourself part of the kingdom by asking God for forgiveness of all your sins and accepting Jesus as your Savior. That will get you reconnected with God and provide you with the greatest blessings that money cannot buy.

We are not preaching just success. We are preaching salvation from an empty barren world to the true blessings of God. Things like real peace and a sound mind can only be found in a relationship with God through Jesus. No money in the world will provide you with the experience of true success.

Divine Capacity: The God Ability that Is in You

79 Making something out of nothing, being able to do more with less, the ability to create; all are traits that identify us with the person of God and His Spirit that He placed in humankind. We often identify ourselves with what we possess in the natural. However, God wants us to identify with Him. Being poor is not in substance; it is in mentality. As someone thinks, the Bible says, so is he or she. It is not the amount of money you have or what you have accomplished. Rather, it is the attitude you have. If you have the knowledge that you have everything, something out of reach will not put you into a panic. We discover who we are and what we have when we are pressed. God has proven who He is in the worst of our situations.

The Multitasking of the Spirit: Focus on Your God-Given Talents

Questions. Is it more important to focus on what you need in a particular aspect of your life or to serve in every position that God has called and equipped you to serve? Is there one thing that you need to focus on, or are there many blessings and opportunities where you may find yourself useful to others? Where should you stop venturing out your talents? What should be ignored on the road to accomplishment?

There are some who are called to do just one thing, and there are others who will not be at peace until they find themselves involved in a multitude of things. If you are a person who feels in your spirit that there is more to do than what you are doing right now, don't tire yourself doing just one thing or having just one job. There is rest in doing the things that you ought to be doing, while you may feel lots of unrest working on just one thing. The secret in finding rest is not to limit yourself in the amount of positions you may occupy. It is in doing all the things that you were born to do. Some received one talent, buried it, and found eternal misery. Others received several talents, make good use of them all, and find eternal joy. Your rest is not in the limited number of things that you must do. Your rest and joy are in the fact that you use all your talents to serve others.

Spirit-Filled Advice about Multitasking

One of the most misused and abused quotes of the Bible by Christians who simply take the Word out of context is this: "I can do all things through Christ who strengthen me" (Philippians 4:13 NKJV). No one can do all things for God has only equipped us to do a limited number of things in limited areas. One needs to perform the duties that suit best his or her talents. In the case of someone holding more than one talent, that person needs to find a position where all those talents can be used to serve others. We are all called to be diligent, whether we have one thing we can do or hold many talents. Don't tire yourself trying to do many things when your God-given ability is to adhere to doing one thing. God knows why you are only able to do just one thing and the intensity of focus it might require from you. Whether it is one or many, do all things with diligence for the glory of God and without being in someone else's way of doing their things. The reward is not for the amount we do but in achieving all that we were called to do.

Pride and Divine Integrity

80 When the moment has called for us to act in all honesty, and we choose to ignore principle and even character for so-called personal gain, we not only deprive ourselves of the integrity that we have from God. We also deprive ourselves of the chance to trust God for what we need.

Integrity is to say no, despite your efforts, after you realize that it's not the right thing to do. Don't move on to defeat and compromise your integrity simply because you have come too far or invested too much time and money to stop. Once you have found that it's wrong, stop and start over. There is such a thing as shameful success.

A divine integrity will help us stand firm before the devil and refuse his offers of a success—at the price of our souls—when only God can guarantee our success.

Pride, on the other hand, is to say no when God Himself has made the opportunity possible because the hard work did not come from us. We cannot refuse to move on to success. Some are so used to hard work that when they find a blessing, they back off from it. If it's not the result of their own sweat, it is

-80-

Don't sell your birthright for a bowl a stew (cf. Genesis 25:27–34).

Pride comes right before the fall (cf. Proverbs 16:18).

not success. God's grace and blessings are the greatest of all successes. You do nothing to deserve it. That kind of success comes to those who trust in God.

You are not to sit in a corner, waiting for God to do for you, when you ought to do for yourself. However, there are times when you will find an opportunity that is completely unexpected. Simply say, "Thank You, Jesus."

Domain 3

Work

Topical biblical references- Chose your favorite bible version to check the following references. The NIV is personally recommended.

-81-

Story of a young man who worked fourteen years for the hand of a young lady in marriage-Cf. Genesis 29:20-30

Work is a continuous effort to achieve a status or a goal. It is the reason humans exist. Work is a service rendered to others. People either work for money or for free, but everyone must work. The opposite of work is stillness, or death—out of service. There are many who occupy themselves with nothing that answers anyone's needs. We are not created to consume life but to work, giving life to great ideas and others.

Economy from a Godly Standpoint

Work should not be an excuse for most people to offer the least of their abilities to make money to spend on what serves absolutely no purpose regarding their destinies.

81 People work. It is an obligation to all who have a sense of responsibility. However, what exactly is considered work, and what is the true purpose behind putting a few hours into doing something, whatever it may be?

To put it more clearly, it is better to give a few examples of where working is the most relevant and very important in someone's advancement.

A young man becomes the age when he would like to take a young woman as a life companion. His life before he made that decision mostly involved his education or maybe helping his parents, doing whatever they wanted him to do. He was a good son to his mother and father, and they enjoyed him as a son. Now that he has decided to choose his own companion, there is one thing that becomes most logical to him and acceptable to all who share his decision. He needs to find a job and work to have the financial means required to sustain himself and his wife-to-be. Regardless of whether he chooses to continue his education, his life now must involve earning money to finance his new desire.

Another example falls in the same category. A young woman aspires to enter a marriage relationship. The man she happens to choose for her husband does not have the financial means to support all that she desires for her new family. She loves the man despite his financial limitation and wants him as her life companion. She will need to do one thing. She needs to find a job and work to help her husband meet the responsibilities of having a family of their own.

One more example is someone with a dream to accomplish something in life. That someone can be of any age or gender. And that dream could be anything from earning a degree or opening a business. Along with the possibility of going to the bank and borrowing the money needed to achieve that dream, that person may also choose to find a job that will help provide the financial means to make that dream become a reality. This person works, saves, and at the end, achieves. That's a great reason to work.

Working, like most things in life, must have a definite purpose attached to it to really benefit from it. Otherwise, all your efforts will contribute to nonsense.

Other Benefits of Working, beyond Finances

82 One gets other benefits from working beyond finances or simply getting a paycheck. Certainly, for the most part, people work for the money. However, not all people work just for that purpose.

Many would like to receive a paycheck without having to wake up every day and deal first with a boss and second, with lazy coworkers, who took the job to get paid but never intended to actually work. We have lots of thieves in the workplace, and truthfully, it is a drag to work with dishonest coworkers. And worse if it happens to be your boss.

In all situations where you must deal with people, the kind of people they are sets the tone and affects your attitude. Whether it is a marriage to one individual or working in a company of dozens of people, you will find more difficulties in dealing with the people involved than with other aspects that come with the situation. Having a great understanding in dealing with people is a blessing. In fact, it is the will of God for people to be able to get along and

-82-

Have a respectable behavior among the unbelievers (cf. 1 Peter 2:12).

Seek also the interests of others while you are seeking for yours (cf. Philippians 2:4)

Do not simply work for food-Cf. John 6:27

Quails and a plague came down on the people God for complaining to God-Cf. Numbers 11:4-6; Numbers 11:31-35

love each other. We are involved with different types of people under many circumstances, but there is no other situation where we are more involved with others than when working directly with others. This is where the greatest commandment is applied, which is to love one another. Practicing the love of God when dealing with others is not an easy task. It is much easier to practice this love when only you and God are involved. People just mess things up. There is no harder experience than working with difficult people and having to love them with the love that God command us to.

God's love is surely the greatest commandment, and the workplace is the biggest field where it's practiced. The love of God is also the way to true success. You cannot succeed while being indifferent to others or having hatred in your heart toward others. You can still make a lot of money mistreating others, but the result is misery. You cannot have a happy life nor experience peace while holding bad sentiment in your heart for others. The practice of love guarantees a better life for those who love and for those being loved. Hence, you can say that the workplace is a perfect training ground to practice the love and righteousness of God. It builds your character while sharpening your skills for better opportunities. Those are really the best benefits of working. The salary you receive is simply a means of exchange to guarantee that you get the equivalent of what you have given to others. The true rewards, however, are from God, who observes how you treat your neighbors in the process of defending your interests.

Humankind Inc.

83 And God said let's create "man" in my image and likeness. The devil's greatest cause of jealousy against humankind has come from the way we were created and the purpose behind our being. We are created in the image of God. We are the only creation in which He placed His own spirit. Nothing can defile us indefinitely. Not even our disobedience toward God is able to separate us from His love for us because He made provision for us to be reconciled with Him through the blood sacrifice of Jesus Christ. We were created earthly with divine capacity, and no one is exempt. Failure is only known to us by us limiting each other. For with the same measure we measure others, we will also be measured. We can only reach the capacity we believe possible for all people.

God loves the ungodly. His love has no limit and, therefore, can be experienced by those who have rejected Him. We must love with the same love that God loves.

Humankind, made in the image of God, is made impossible to fail but easy to distract. We may hold the power to achieve all things but waste our time and energy on achieving foolish goals. Humans, created in the image of God, have spent most of their energy trying to prove their capabilities to other humans who are also created in the same image. We were created to achieve great things, and to place our greatness at the service to each other, not to prove ourselves to another. We do not all possess the same gifts, but every person's gift is the opportunity not to boost

By the same limit you give to others you also set your own limit (cf. Matthew 7:2).

Bear each other's burden as God requires of us (cf. Galatians 6:2–5).

Do your best to present yourself to God as one approved (cf. 2 Timothy 2:15).

our egos or prove ourselves to others. Rather, your personal gifts are your opportunity to participate and grow as part of the family of humankind. You were born great and accomplished. Nothing you do will make you any greater than the day you first showed up on this planet. It is a waste to try to achieve greatness beyond ourselves. We are not to prove ourselves but simply to present ourselves.

What Do We Make of People Who Are Poor or Destitute in Society?

-84-
Bless and do not curse (cf. Romans 12:14).

84 In the race for proving ourselves to ourselves, many have believed in the lie of being inferior to others at some point in their lives. In the course of the journey to find ourselves, some of us have been made to believe that we are slow, stupid, or inferior. And the power of a person's word over another to bless one another has been used in reverse. So we have placed many under a psychological and mental curse by the words we used toward them. Those of us who have been encouraged by either great teachers or parents in our lives need to return that favor to others who also need words of blessing and encouragement to break curses in their lives. Every person well-nourished by the appropriate words of blessing and encouragement can be trained to serve society in one's created greatness. There is no such thing as a stupid person, but there is a curse that can make you believe you are. And as one thinks, one is. Therefore, many have been made incapable in our society by the curses of our mouths.

What Do We Make of the Gifted in the World's Society?

85 The key word is "gifted." Everyone is gifted in ways that are different from others. Some gifts are made to be opened in public; some are not. I have heard of some men and women who are very gifted in bed. Those individuals simply have the ability of giving that kind of pleasure to anyone blessed to receive that service from them. It is, however, a service that is limited to one or maybe two individuals in their entire lifetimes. Although a great service, but not too many (I hope) will come to experience that great service from those individuals.

However, we have other gifts and talents that are made to serve a larger group of people. We also have talents with the only purpose being to help other talents be known and discovered by others who may need them. For instance, a group of talents put together and known as publishing made this book possible for others to read. Although this book may be known by many, the name of other talents involved may never be known, like the author. Does it matter that your talent is never to be known by the public? No, unless you are in the service of proving yourself to others. It should only matter that we serve others with our gifts. It is also a great blessing to be surrounded by a small group who truly loves us than to be known by many but truly loved by no one.

What Are Educational Institutions Good For?

-86-

The basics of human intelligence, your IQ and your EQ:

Recommend reading The EQ Edge: Emotional Intelligence and Your Success, written by Steven J. Stein PhD and Howard E. Book MD.

One might also want to read the Millionaire Mind by Thomas Stanley. All are documents used to research for this book.

Others able to teach others (cf. 2 Timothy 2:2).

86 Educational institutions are there to help us cultivate our talents and help us become better servants to each other. Schooling is not made to sell us programs or curriculums. The most talented mechanic can go through medical school and graduate with honors simply because the individual has a brain and learning ability. However, the individual's joy and talent as a mechanic would better serve the community. As a mechanic, work and passion would never have to be separated. That person would be a better servant to the world's society. The mechanic would not dread going to work and competing with others who may also be trying to prove themselves in unknown territories. We are more confident in our own skin, doing what we are best at.

But educational institutions also support the false ideology of comparing one individual with another. They also believe some are smarter than others when, in reality and biblically, this is not the case. Some are more prone to receiving information than others. Relatively, that may be the reality of this matter. A single means used to transmit information may not be the best for everyone. Everyone learns at his or her own pace, and we may more quickly capture information that pertains to what interests us. The fact that someone doesn't grasp information fast enough may be because he or she has no interest in what is being taught. Change the field of study, and maybe that will make a difference.

Totally Different Smarts

The most commonly used individual IQ tests in the United States and other English-speaking countries are the Stanford-Binet-5 (SB5) and the Wechsler Intelligent Test series that include a scale for adult and another scale for children. Any simple internet or google search will lead you directly to those two. But, just to be on the same page with everyone, let's ask this question. What is an IQ? The Intelligence Quotient or IQ is how you measure how fast or how slow an individual is, brain wise. That is my version. The simplest definition from Doctors Steven Stein and Howard Book, two well-known doctors on the matters of IQ and its testing is this; *"IQ is a measure of an individual's intellectual, analytical, logical and rational abilities. As such, it's concerned with verbal, spatial, visual and mathematical skills. It gauges how readily we learn new things; focus on tasks and exercises; retain and recall objective information; engage in a reasoning process; manipulate numbers; think abstractly as well as analytically; and solve problems by the applications of prior knowledge."* In short, the IQ is how you differentiate the smart people from those who are not so smart. That was before they discovered different kind of smarts.

IQ testing has been around since Before Christ. But no need to go that far back to make my point. In 1940 David Wechsler, the clinical psychologists with Bellevue Hospital who is responsible for the originally known Wechsler-Bellevue Intelligence Scales, argued that other factors needed to be considered in the test to complete the overall view of the measurement. Factors that include confidence, the fear of failure, and attitude. However, those are considered emotional factors and therefore did not make the test. IQ is based on cognitive intelligence or brain smarts. The part of the brain responsible for that kind of intelligent is called the cortex. It is also the part of the brain that they find is thicker or larger in women than men, but we'll leave that for another discussion. It is my opinion that emotional factors could not be considered in the same test as cognitive factors, because different parts of the brain are responsible for the two groups. In 1948, a researcher named R.W. Leeper has singled out the emotional factors as "Emotional thoughts" but few psychologists were interested in that sort of studies. Later in the year 1990, a few doctors and researchers and just to name a few; Albert Ellis, Howard Gardner of Harvard University, Reuven Bar-On, John Mayer of the University of New Hampshire, and Peter Salovey of Yale University; with the contributions of those scientists, what was formerly known as "Street smarts" and "Common sense" has been proven to be another type of intelligence now widely recognized as "EQ" Emotional Quotient with its own developed method of testing called "EQ-i". Now what makes EQ so interesting is that common sense has been around since the beginning of time, it simply never been recognized officially as a form of intelligence. And better yet it involves some very important aspect of human subsistence and personal development like confidence or faith, the ability to get along with others or the practice of tolerance or love. Also, according to experts on the matter, your high score of IQ does not say that you will be successful in life, or that you will be able to perform greatly at work. When your EQ, on the hand can be considered to determine from 27 to 45 percent your chances to be a success at your job. With that being said, we can all agree that unless an individual is medically challenged to the extreme, we can all contribute to the advancement of our society using our God given smarts. The biblical truth is that everyone will be taken accountable before God for what they have done with their talents and abilities to serve their neighbours. In a book called *Millionaire Mind* by an American bestselling author named Thomas Stanley, a few millionaires who became by profession or their business owners, have declared that they have always wondered how they could reach their success, since they were told by authorities in the educational system that they were not success materials. The truth is, it does matter if anyone has told you that you are stupid, if you do not succeed in life it is not because it is true, but it is rather because you believed in the lie.

-87-

Great are those who consider these things (Romans 12:16; 1 Corinthians 10:24; Philippians 2:3, 5–7; Mark 10:45; Colossians 3:23; Galatians 5:13, 22–23; Ephesians 4:31–32; Romans 12:10; Luke 22:27; 1 John 4:8).

Doing Life Together

87 It is by the weakness of the people you may have carried that your strengths are revealed for many to see. God has placed you and them together to do life.

The will of God is for us to be a support system for each other. No one has it all together without the help of someone else. Whatever glory you may claim for yourself it directly attributable to the experiences you build up from being with others. One cannot pride himself or herself by claiming to be self-made. We are the products of many who have contributed their efforts to our lives. The good and the bad that happened to us are all packaged together to make us who we are. The only one you can credit for making you the great person you are is God, who used your worst experiences in your favor. We could all be destroyed by what happens to us during our lives. But God made it so we not only forgive our offenders but use the bad experience to help others who are going through similar situations.

In an executive office in Boston, Massachusetts, I have read on a poster, "In life, it's 10% what happens to you, and 90% how you take it." Don't let the worst experience in your life ruin you. Learn to use these experiences to help others have more hope and know for sure that everything will be all right. There is life after failure. And the advantage we have after having a bad experience is the knowledge that such a bad experience is possible, and something must be done to prevent it. We are together in this thing called life. We can act like we are different than everyone else, or we can share with others the good and the bad we have all experienced. That would help us to grow stronger as a people and a world.

To Live by Faith and Not by Fear

88 The Bible says the just shall live by his faith. I see things and envision the future as God wants me to live. And yes, it might require that we endure much to achieve the dreams God revealed to us. But His promises guarantee a coming reality we have as an exclusive benefit. The world does not guarantee us victory. Not even hard work can guarantee anyone prosperity. Only those who trust in God have the peace of mind and the principles to prevent them from not selling out to the devil and cause others to suffer so they succeed or achieve their goals in life.

The world presents life to us as a race, a struggle, or a hustle. We are not to hustle in life or even need to race with others to achieve the same dreams and occupy the same positions. We are not called to the same purposes in life. And although we have to submit to each other on occasion, we are never to conceive in our minds the thought of being superior to another. We all carry authority in our callings. And though many show weaknesses in the endeavors they were called to perform, we are not to deprive anyone of their right to be a leader on his or her turfs. Let God be the judge of the bad leadership of others. Be the perfect leader in what you do at the time God permits you to be.

There is no reason for anyone to be jealous of anyone else once they know they have their own paths and fields to cultivate. Time is short enough for us to achieve our missions on earth and share with others whatever goodness God has placed in us. Jealousy against our brethren is mere distraction on the road to our own achievements in life. We can and will get to our destinations without having to fight someone else for the spot he or she already occupies.

We could have all been trained for the same position in the same field, but we have been called to perform different assignments. And we all will

-89-

The diligent gets the precious wealth (cf. Proverbs 12:27).

Into service to others the gift that have received from God (cf. 1 Peter 4:10).

have to submit to each other at one time or another. Do not foul yourselves by thinking you're on top and everyone else at the bottom. You are the only one on top of your own assignment, which you need to complete. The respect you have for others determines how well you will achieve. Everyone can make something happen, but not all will have the reward and credit of an assignment well done. If you must sacrifice your respect for others to make something happen, you are not operating by faith but by fear. Many fear they might never achieve their own potential. Therefore, they dedicate their lives to the devil's plan to ruin others. Fearful people are miserable and dangerous people. But those who live by faith are no better than anyone else. Rather, they are sources of strength and encouragement to all.

Be Where You Are Needed— Be Your Own Boss

89 "You can go anytime now, Lee," said the young supervisor.

"We will be very strict on people punching out for lunch," another one said. As for Mr. Longtime Kitchen Boss, if you have time to stand to talk to anyone other than him, it is time for you to go home.

All those people have control over your coming in and going out of work, meaning that they have control over your livelihood and how much you should earn on their watch. The truth is that someone placed them in the position to watch over someone else's earnings. That makes them responsible as controllers to tell others how much labor they need from them and the quality of that labor. It is an awesome amount of control to give someone over you. Everyone's level of productivity should be under their own control, and no one should have authority over the amount of work someone should put in daily.

Work is sacred. It is how humankind freely contributes to society. It's how we serve each other. The more control you have over your work and level of productivity, the better hand you have over your prosperity and happiness. When it comes to how much money you should make, you need to ask yourself how much you are willing to put in. And to have control over your goal, you first need to have control over the amount of labor you want to contribute and your earnings for that labor. You need to be your own boss. You need to have more control over your talents and the services you have to offer and share those talents to as many as possible. You need not to depend on one source of income. Cultivate as many as possible from different means and talents. You need to keep active. Lots of bible verses supports the idea of being productive and diligent. Proverbs 12:27 (NKJV); Proverbs 10:4; Proverbs 13:4

From kindergarten to the guiding counselor's office, all the way to the human resources office, no one has your best interest in mind than yourself. You are your best free agent. Although you may find others to motivate and guide you through becoming the best service provider you can, you need to know what you want out of your limited time on this earth. You do not need to be a doctor; or maybe you do. The earlier you find out what you want to do, and the sooner you discover your talents, the better your chances are for you to make something valuable out of yourself. Maybe you need to play an instrument. Your way into your destiny may be a book or an old guitar. Whatever it is that got your attention, you need to be dedicated to it to use it as a way out for yourself and others. Something is particular to every individual living on the planet. It is necessary for each of us to discover what it is. You dedicated work and talent will give you the control you need over your livelihood and then your productivity, next your dream, and finally your destiny. Invest some valuable time and dedication to your dreams. Don't be a scoffer. Don't spend time doing foolishness, whatever that foolishness maybe.

I was often sent home early or cut off the schedule due to high labor. Meaning that there are more employees present than there are customers to receive the service that the business is offering. Although I felt insulted every time, I always understood the responsibility managers had to control their labor. I wasn't upset with them. I was rather upset with myself, knowing the capacity that I have and the things that I could do to give me unlimited possibility to create my own income and wealth.

It is a free world out there, and no one should solely work for someone else. There are plenty of opportunities to be of service to others as a free agent. You simply must focus on discovering your talents, and work hard and smart to achieve your desired success.

Domain 4

Wealth

Topical biblical references: Choose your favorite Bible version to check the following references. The NIV is personally recommended.

-90-

True wealth is found in placing your complete trust in God and His Word (cf. Jeremiah 9:23–24).

Wealth is considered the abundance in all that is valuable, or in money. Affluence is great wealth. A good reputation is also great wealth. Wealth is often measured in cash in our world societies, but it goes far beyond money. Where favor and talents are the currency, money is not needed and, therefore, has no value. However, where money is the currency, you will still need talents or maybe a favor.

True Wealth Is an Everyday Blessing

The essence of these texts is to enumerate on the daily blessings and how God truly renews our strength every morning. Every day is truly a new day, and one way to secure the grace of God every day in our lives is to make Him the boss of our lives. We can live free to enjoy life in abundance, but we must live and be in Jesus.

90 No one knows what tomorrow will bring and how it will be. Today may not be the end of a lot of things in your life concerning your financial status or health, but it certainly is the end of yesterday in many aspects. Every day is a chance for everyone to repent of what in their lives is not right and take a new, positive direction to be and do better. Every day is a chance for everyone to grow.

Many have often had the opportunity to grasp the knowledge beyond all knowledge and the peace that surpasses all understanding. Every day there is a chance for everyone to acknowledge the grace of God and a chance to make the decision to walk with God. Everyone has faith in something, and most have faith in themselves to make what they hope to come to life. Walking with God simply switch one's faith from whatever it may be on to God, who is the source of all things. God gives all things and truly. Peace is not guaranteed with anything anyone may have without God, so everything needs to come from Him. All our hopes need to be in Him.

What Is Being Rich or Wealthy?

91 There is an extremely big difference between being wealthy and having a lot of money. Someone who has a lot money is not necessarily wealthy or rich. And I am not talking about being poor in spirit. Money is simply a commodity. It is a means of exchange. Someone who has a lot of money only has the ability to exchange his or her money with another person who has a service or product to offer. The rich person in this situation is the person with the service or product to offer. Money itself has no power and no use without those to offer the products and services that we need. Real wealth and riches are in the hands of those who have something to offer. The more someone has to offer, the wealthier that person is, whether or not that person chooses to exchange those gifts for money. Many die rich or wealthy without ever making a dime from what they could offer society. God is completely against that. At the same time, there are those who offer nothing of good value yet profit much in cash value for their nonsense contribution.

Most people who aspire to having a lot of money are the same ones who do not want to be of service to others. The secret to real wealth is not to aspire to have money but to dream of what good you can do to serve others in your community and the world. On judgment day, God will not ask you how much money you made. But He will certainly ask you what you did with your talents and all the opportunities you had to serve others while you were alive.

Spirit-Filled Advice about Wealth

Everyone is born with a source of wealth that is under attack from the day they were born. This wealth is known as the wealth of spiritual identity. It is said in the Bible that humankind was created in the image of God. Nothing anyone owns will be worth more than this fact and privilege. We are not the only beings ever created. Apart from everything created on this planet, there are other beings created in the heavens long before us. Although they are powerful due to how they were made and their positions, they were not created in the image of God. And one of those powerful beings is madly jealous of us.

What does it mean to be created in the resemblance of God? It may not mean much to us humans, but to the heavenly beings, it is a powerful knowledge they are willing to dedicate their entire existence to keep us ignorant of. Being created like God means that we have creative power, like God, however to the limit that He sets. And from what humankind has been able to achieve, I would say that God has allowed us to create much.

We have a powerful enemy who can only win by using us against us. The greatest strategy used by that enemy is to lead us to believe that we are relatively inferior or made less valuable than another. We may have been born socially and economically less fortunate and with different challenges, but we are all created to thrive. True wealth is not how you were born or what you were able to accumulate through generations. It is in how you were created in God's own image. Let no one tell you that you hold less value than that.

Topical biblical references- Chose your favorite bible version to check the following references. The NIV is personally recommended.

Domain 5

Money

-92-

Example of a master who paid all his employees the same, regardless of the number of hours they each worked-Cf. Matthew 20:1-16 -

Money does not satisfy those who love it-Cf. Ecclesiastes 5:10; Isaiah 55:2

Money in the hands of fool the bible says is not worth much-Cf. Proverbs 17:16

Money is nothing but a way of making an exchange more easily. The value is not in the coin or the bill itself. The true value of the money is in the good or service offered in exchange.

The Value of Money

92 What does your money represent? What is the value of what you do for others, and how did they come to that evaluation? How is it that two people are doing the exact same work, and one happens to receive more in salary than the other? And the one who receives the least could be the one that is more productive. What does money really represent in the world society, and how much importance must one place in making money?

One of the most undeniable truths to consider is that just as sex deviates the true value of the relationship between men and women, money deviates true value and importance in human

-93-

How much money would someone give in exchange for his soul? (cf. Luke 12:13–21).

Redemption was not at the cost of silver or gold (cf. 1 Peter 1:18–19).

relationships. The knowledge of sex and sexuality was created by God to unite the man and the woman in an intimate relationship to accomplish God's design for humankind. However, the concept of money and the way it is utilized is not from God. Just like sex is the most intimate connection in the male and female relationship, money is the greatest commodity in business exchange among humans. The reward is in their good rapport and perfect understanding of each other. In the same way sexual intercourse in the absence of love is empty, money without fellowship among us humans is also empty.

The Insufficiency of Funds

93 Not having enough money to make an exchange on a specific level is a problem all people have, regardless of financial worth. Everyone will sometimes require a service of some kind or want to purchase something for which they have not worked enough to acquire. No one will ever reach the level of wealth or credit to be able to access by means of money everything needed. Although everything seems to have come with a price tag, and life may seem impossible without money, many of the greatest things in the world cannot be purchased with cash. Therefore, why is money so much an issue? If money does not satisfy those who have plenty of it, why is it that many are focused so intensely on making as much money as possible? What is it in being rich that attracts those who do not have so much money? The best answer is rest.

People simply work so much that they feel the need to take a break from hard labor. They need some money, so they have time to enjoy the loved ones a little. The need is so strong that Jesus offered it as an incentive to join Him as a disciple. He said, "Come to me those who are tired and heavy laden, and I will give you rest." Matthew 11:28. So many are working so hard, yet their needs still cannot be met. People either are working too much or not working at all. There seems to be no balance between the two.

There are enough talents in the world and enough product to serve every human being on this planet. The only shortcoming in our lack of service to others is caused by selfishness and greed in the system of exchange. We all want to be rich as fast as we can and worse, save as much as we can in order not to offer ourselves of service to others. The result of that is inflation. Too much money and not enough services offered.

The world industry believes in making great profits, not in taking care of those producing the profits. You find the workload of five people being placed on the shoulders of one person only to maximize profit. Labor cutting is one of the greatest causes of unemployment in the world. It's not that they don't need people. It's that their focus is too much on marginalizing their staff for the sake of profit. Plenty of money is made and saved, but people are starving everywhere. It is not that we suffer lack of cash or talents. The greatest lack humanity suffers is the lack of conscience.

On the Issue of Money

Come Jesus said and I will give you rest-Cf. Matthew 11:28

A biblical warning to the rich oppressors- Cf. James 5:1-6; Proverbs 14:31

-94-

The parable of talents-Cf. Matthew 25:14-30

To labor in vain-Cf. Psalm 127:1-2

A godly message to the thieves-Cf. Ephesians 4:28

A divine message to the scoffers-Cf. Proverbs 12:27

94 The parable of talents tells us how the master gave each of his three servants a different number of talents and how they all, except one, brought him back interest on their investments of those talents. The one who did not bring anything to his master was asked to be sent in the lake of fire. In other words, he was sent to hell for not investing his talents.

The Bible is pretty clear on the fact that we must place ourselves in service to others, and this story told by Jesus, tells us our talents must provide us and our Master, who is God, with great profits in return. But what are our talents, and what do we do with them?

The most common excuse used by those who do not invest in others using their talents is that they do not have any talents. The second one is that no one will support them or pay money for what they have to offer. Most people simply use their most valuable assets as hobbies and claim nothing for their efforts using them. They do not take seriously what God has given them, so they do not feel the obligation to work at being great at their purposes in life. If misery is not described as waking up to doing what you hate, maybe it should. The greatest number of heart attacks was once noted as occurring on Monday mornings to people obligated to go to a job they did not like. Most people work doing something that will take them nowhere. Every day they walk that path to their own destruction. They do it for the money. There has to be a means of earning a leaving, no matter how difficult it may be. But most are earning that living at the cost of their own breaths. And all are consequences for taking one's talents for granted.

Work brings up the issue of money, and money has become the focus behind work. People have done things for others way before the existence of money. We cannot make money the reason we do things for others. You may wonder how you will be able to purchase the things needed to survive. We must work to acquire the things that we need. The point is not that we should not get paid for the services we render to others. Rather, the point is that we must be generous to those we serve and those who help us be of service to others. Use the talents you have to serve others and as much as you can, volunteer your service, expect nothing from those you serve in return. Do not hide your talents and expect a reward from the Master who gave them to you. Have fun doing what you enjoy doing. You never know who will benefit from it. Do not always make money the issue.

Spirit-Filled Advice about Money and Your Talents

If one has not yet failed doing what the person was called to do, he or she has yet never failed. However, individuals must not fear using their talents. Rather, they should fear the consequences that come from not using them. One was not created to make money but to be of service to others using all his or her talents. Yes, money might come as the result of using one's talents to serve others, but the greatest satisfaction will not be from the exchange of currencies. The greatest satisfaction comes from the need others have for the service or product coming from the use of those talents. People strive for the need to be needed. Not being needed in the society where one lives can lead to madness. Fortunately, everyone is needed for we all have something the world needs from us. And that need is our effort to help someone with a need we can fill. It may be small, the need that one fills, but to those with the need, it is nothing small. We are to do the best we can with what we have, and God is responsible to make it great before others. Money should never be our focus in doing anything. Rather our focus must be on what needs to be done.

Domain 6

Justice (Peace)

The word "justice" commonly implies an outcome, the result of a wrongdoing one has suffered, the final decision of the judge or jury in a criminal case. Not many consider justice as the word truly means. Justice does not happen at the end but at the beginning in human relations. Justice is an attitude or treatment; it is not a verdict. In your relationship with others every day, you get to either practice justice or evil toward them. Your verdict and judgment regarding others are significant in the way you treat them. Your treatment, however, is more important to prove the justice that you practice yourself. Doing someone justice is treating them as you would want to be treated. God's justice in you will keep you from His judgment.

Introductory Note

If the justice of God and His judgment appear ridiculous to most, it is simply because God does not see things and situations through human eyes. We

Topical biblical references: Chose your favorite Bible version to check the following references. The NIV is personally recommended.

Introductory Note

God's precepts are right, and His decrees are firm (cf. Psalm 19:9).

God has a better view of all your situations, and better solutions (cf. Isaiah 55:8; Psalm 115:3; Psalm 135:6).

God asked His people where they were when He was creating heaven and earth (Cf. Job 38:4).

The law of sowing and reaping (cf. Galatians 6:7; Job 4:8).

The law of seed time and harvest (cf. Genesis 8:22).

To love our enemies (cf. Matthew 5:44; Luke 6:27–36).

judge things differently than God does. The justice of God is not always fair, and at times, it seems too slow to humankind. The Creator of the universe is sovereign and omnipotent, so He does what He desires to do. That doesn't mean, for example, that God doesn't have justice in Him. It simply means that the One who created the entire universe will not always do what, in our judgment, appears to be the right thing at the time. We do not understand everything. So when God comes to certain conclusions in our lives that are not pleasant, we may choose to deny the existence of the Almighty based on ignorance and how we feel at the moment. Since we do not have all the information, we simply assume that the outcome cannot be to our advantage and become upset at God, who has our best interests in mind all the time.

God is the author and the only one with the knowledge of all things happening on the earth and in the heavens. He gives us limited knowledge on things, so we may be able to manipulate the affairs both on earth, and in heaven. God has given us access to part of His knowledge to function like the supreme beings we are. One does not even have to believe in God to use and benefit from His knowledge. However, if you do believe in God and trust Him in all your affairs, you will know the greatest success.

There is much divine knowledge common to all beings and used by multitudes of people in all cultures. We have, for instance, knowledge of the law of reciprocity, otherwise known as the law of giving and receiving. Everyone in every culture can relate to this law. This law guarantees that anyone you give something to will naturally feel the obligation to give you something back. Another well-known law is the law of positive thinking, otherwise known as the law of attraction. This law tells you what has been written in your Holy Bible for centuries: "As a man think, so is he."

Some people live in the negative, and no doubt they wonder how their lives always turn out so miserable and negative. The key to this law is explained a bit more in this book in text number 33, "Christianity Concerning the Key Aspects of the Human Race." This law explains how your entire life is wrapped around your belief system and how a positive attitude about yourself and others can create a far better outcome, thus, a better living atmosphere for everyone.

It is the same for the justice of God. There is a set of laws in place to activate appropriate rewards and consequences for each of our actions. It is not God who directly punishes us for what we do wrong; rather, our actions put us under God's judgment and cause us to suffer the consequences of our wrongdoings. Consequently, it is in our best interests to act in love, which is the only applicable law there is. This law tells us to love God and to love everyone, even those we consider enemies. Love, the Bible says, covers a multitude of wrongdoings, ours and others. He who acts in love, the Bible implies, accomplishes all the laws.

We cannot fall under any condemnation if we practice the love of God. Your motive will always be good toward everyone. But if anyone nourishes evil, which is all kind of selfish motives, toward others,

Topical biblical
references: Chose
your favorite Bible
version to check the
following references.
The NIV is personally
recommended.

that person will fall under God's judgment and will pay the consequences.

Do Not Participate in the Sins of Others

-95-

God will fight your battles, but you must keep your peace (cf. Exodus 14:14).

95 You will often be invited to either experience anger and other negative attitudes of others. Do not touch it. Don't let yourself be tempted. Don't let what someone either says or does to you make you upset or turn your mood negative. Let the judgment of God rule in your favor. It is written in your Christian Bible that "The Lord will fight for you; and you shall hold your peace." Exodus 14:14 (NKJV)

It is the grace of God to suffer affliction unjustly (cf. 1 Peter 2:19).

God intends for us to be at peace and enjoy His blessings. When someone without the knowledge of God and under the influence of evil comes to you with an attitude or anger, you must know it is spiritual warfare, and you will not win if you're have the same attitude as the other person. In fact, no one wins fighting evil with evil. Instead, use the principle of love that says love forgives all. And respond, if you must, in a manner that promotes peace.

God's justice and judgment are automatic. Do not find yourself doing things that will place you under God's judgment.

The Circle of Great Confusion:
Do Not Argue Differences

96 One who has ears to hear, let hear. The worst you can do to yourself regarding rapport with others is to argue differences. Let your rights be taken by others without the need of an explanation. There is no need for others to ever understand our goodness. We do not need to explain our kindness to others. We simply need to let our goodness be known to others, and if someone happens not to understand it, let it be taken for granted. It is God who will reward us for the kindness we show to all.

Peace is found in a sacrifice we haven't made ourselves. It is given to everyone by Jesus, who is the only provider of genuine peace. He was the only one qualified to make the sacrifice, and He did to redeem us from the turmoil of disobedience toward God. For us to benefit from the sacrifice Jesus made and be able to enjoy that genuine peace, we must follow His principles and the way of life set before us in the Holy Scriptures. This way of life is what is called the righteousness of God.

This righteousness is not a set of rules we simply need to follow. It is a complete understanding of and wisdom about a relationship with God, the Creator, and all His creations. The righteousness of God is how to relate with God and operate in His blessings. It is a complete understanding of life itself.

"So then, my beloved brethren, let every man be swift to hear, slow to speak, slow to wrath; for the wrath of man does not produce the righteousness of God." James 1:19-20 (NKJV)

Our madness in the way we understand and settle our matters does not produce the same result as when we apply the righteousness of God. So to know the genuine peace of God, we need to apply God's principles. There is a way to settle our differences and have peace, but we must be willing to step into His righteousness, not our own.

Domain 7

Church

-97-

Topical biblical references: Choose your favorite Bible version to check the following references. The NIV is personally recommended.

A church used to be a dedicated building where God meets with His people to receive their offerings and sacrifices. Now the church is no more a building; it is the person disciple of Jesus Christ. The church is the Christian himself or herself. God is now worshipped in spirit and in truth, not at a dedicated place. God is found anywhere His name is glorified.

Pay no mind to those who observe worshipping on certain days and in certain places (Cf. Romans 14:5–6; John 4:21–23).

Church and Godliness

97 There is a kind of godliness that is not at all godly. Such godliness is the practice of religion. Jesus told Peter that he is a rock, and upon that rock the church of Jesus is built. The gates of hell, Jesus said, cannot prevail against it. The church Jesus built is a strong and very powerful institution that is the house of God. Many others have since built churches. However, it is said in the Word of God that if God does not build the house, those who build do it in vain. So we have many places we call church, but they are not in God's plan.

Masters upon Masters: The Reign of False Prophets

-98-

Be aware of vain builders (cf. Psalm 127:1).

No flesh will glory before God (cf. 1 Corinthians 1:29–31).

To be light and salt is the call of God to the church (cf. Matthew 5:13–16; Ephesians 5:8).

Masters upon masters, all based on the preference of the audiences (cf. 2 Timothy 4:3).

98 Jesus said many would come in His name. Many it is, and the demand for more of those false prophets makes them keep coming. People having problems hearing the true gospel is why we have diversity in the gospel and different doctrines that stand against the Word of God. People need the blessings and the glory of God while they are still operating in the flesh. They crave the blessings and the glory of God even while they still want to live according to their own understanding. And no flesh will be glorified before God, says the Word of God.

The spirit of God has a different set of understandings than what the spirit of humankind can understand. God operates in love, while humankind operates in pride. The major part of the difference is that love is humble and serving, but pride is boastful and demanding. Jesus is, for us, the greatest example of love. He who descended from heaven to us in a spirit of service, although being served by angels Himself, never prided Himself as being too important to serve those far inferior to Him. This kind of serving spirit does not inspire many who are looking to be served. The spirit and the gospel of Jesus will never be appealing to those whose hearts are proud, selfish, and attached to the things of this world. Those who wish to be blessed and glorified by God but will not do the things of God require more of the knowledge of God to benefit themselves. However, God's true prophets cannot prophesy any lies. Those people will need their own teachers to tell them that God will honor them without having to deny themselves of their pride and desires of the flesh.

"For the time will come when they will not endure sound doctrine, but according to their own desires, because they have itching ears, they will heap up for themselves teachers; and they will turn their ears away from the truth, and be turned aside to fables." 2 Timothy 4:3-4 (NKJV)

More time is spent straightening out the family of God than to make a difference in the world. The church does not seem to realize that the more confusion in the family, greater is the victory on the side of evil. The need for Christians to submit to the authority of the Word of God and start to practice it cannot be emphasized enough if the church is to represent the kingdom of God in the world today. We cannot do as they do and expect them to see us as different than them.

The only difference between those who do and those who can is that the ones who do, simply do; and those who can, judge and criticize. Faith is justified by good works, not words. Get with the program of God. Be the light and salt of the earth for the world to see and follow.

Spirit-Filled Advice about Heresy

One is not to confuse the true gospel of Jesus with the enormous number of gospels invading our world society. Heresy has been a problem since the beginning, when Eve was tempted in the garden of Eden by the devil. "Does God really say," is asked by the enemy to animate doubt in the hearts of those in whom the Word of God has been planted. One cannot stop the work of evil, especially that of spreading false teaching among the people of God. We are in a world ruled by evil. We are under the empire of the evil one, and it is evident that God will not prevent His people from being influenced or tempted by the dark world. It is in the power of those who believe in God to stand firm on the truth and reject everything that stands against the knowledge received from God through His prophets. We are not to focus on the lies told by those led by the spirit of confusion. Our focus is to be on the true knowledge of God to help us discern the lies when we come face to face with those who prophesy lies. And as the example of Jesus Himself, when anyone approaches us with the spirit of confusion—even when they would use God's own Word—we will be able to use the same Word to clear any doubt about what God has really said to us. As the devil kept saying to Jesus, "It is written." Jesus kept answering, "It is also written." Knowledge is the only way to fight ignorance.

Domain 9

Sex/Mating

The simplest definition of sex/mating is the coming together of two animals of the same species to breed. For humans, sex is the closest bond reserved for two people, a man and a woman who wish to commit to each other for life as husband and wife. Sex is not made to happen between people who simply consider themselves friends. Sex is the act of being connected for life.

Made with Purpose

99 A man was created for the purpose to serve God and his neighbor. The woman was created for the purpose to help the man. For a woman to serve her true purpose, a man who is her husband must consider her part of his own. He needs to love and care for her both in the natural and spiritual. The only self-indulgence God allows to a man has to do with his wife. He who he indulges himself in the love for his wife indulges in the love for himself. The same love

Topical biblical references: Choose your favorite Bible version to check the following references. The NIV is personally recommended.

-99-

The purpose of man and the woman God gave him (cf. Isaiah 43:7; Ephesians 5:28; 2:10).

Women are created equal to men and because of men (cf. Genesis 2:18).

The wife is to be subject to her husband for the sake of the kingdom of God (cf. 1 Peter 3:1).

The immeasurable love of the husband for his wife (cf. Ephesians 5:25–33).

is compared with the love of Jesus for the church; He loved it so much that He died on the cross. This is the love God requires a husband to have for his wife. A very intense and true love it is.

Sex is scientifically proven the greatest preoccupation of men's minds. In the presence of a female, especially one who flaunts her sexuality in the least manner, a normally brain wired man will quickly and naturally jumped into sex mode. Due to a physical part of the human brain called the nucleus accumbens, part of the reward circuit, a man will have a natural reaction towards a woman like he wants this. He will feel sexual towards any physically desirable female. That is more explained in a book called *Through a man's eyes* written by Shaunti Feldhahn and Craig Gross. However, sex is also the most misinterpreted need known to humankind. Sex is a service not to men but to women and begins not at intercourse but in the way a man treats a woman. Our society considers a short moment of this long-term treatment as foreplay. Most women let their men get away with enjoying themselves at their expense because they figure that men simply are selfish and that they can never understand why women are seldom in the mood for sex. However, the fact that a woman lets a man jump on her without him meeting her required natural and spiritual needs makes her a prostitute. This simply means someone who sell herself short. Most men treat their women as such. They simply want their wives to give it to them without meeting their most important needs—the need for women to feel safe, secure, and loved. You provide that to her and she will not only give you the greatest experience that God wanted you to have, she will also be the help she was meant to be.

Running a Bicycle with One Wheel Flat

100 Two is better than one. However, both must be in great shape. Many husbands have been running their families with a flat tire a long time and wonder why they are not going anywhere fast enough. Women are not stupid or crazy. In fact, they are scientifically proven more apt to solve problems better and faster than men. Based on a research led by a psychologist named Stuart Ritchie, a postdoctoral gentleman at the University of Edinburgh in the United Kingdom, they found that women tend to have significantly thicker cortices than men. Now thicker cortices or the brain cortex is responsible for a high score of IQ on many cognitive intelligence tests. That scientifically makes women smarter than men - brain wise. The problem is most women are simply not satisfied. They have been providing men with great pleasure since Adam laid eyes on Eve for the first time. However, few women have experienced the love they should from those who owe it to them. Parents, take great care of your children; husbands, love your wives. That is all prescribed by God in the Bible.

It is not for no reason that God created men to have such a strong physical and emotional attraction for women. Something must be up with that. It is not that all men are perverted, but sex has been reduced to

-100-

Two are better than one (cf. Ecclesiastes 4:9–12).

Scientific document used for research (Sciencemag.org / scientific report written by Michael Price dated April 11, 2017).

just sexual intercourse. Sex however begins with the initial desire a man has for a certain woman, and the woman who that man craves for will give meaning to that desire. The woman is the one responsible to make the man fulfill all the requirements that come with such a craving. She and her moral or spiritual values determine whether she will have cheap sexual intercourse with the man who wants her. Or will she make him respond to all the requirements before satisfying that passion of his? The woman is the commanding officer when it comes to a man who desires anything from her. Our Christian bible requires that the woman must first make the man go through the practice of love before she lets him lay hands on her. No intercourse should happen before a man goes through the proper channel of taking a woman in marriage. Otherwise, she prostitutes herself and causes the man to value her less.

The female population is great in the world, but that doesn't mean women have become less valuable. What has really become less valuable is their moral or spiritual value in our societies. A woman who doesn't know her real value will sell herself cheap, and men will treat her as a sex object. That is not part of God's plan for women.

A man who does not understand the real value of all women will not consider that of his wife. Knowledge is key in all situations. In this case, a man needs to learn why the Bible says God created women and the attitude the Almighty has toward His precious female creatures. One cannot fully be satisfied using an instrument that he does not know how to use. The same for a man who believes the only reason God created woman is for sexual use. He will not run well with a woman by his side. He will also lose out on the greatest gift and blessing that God has given to a man: woman.

Spirit-Filled Advice about Having a Mate

The Bible states that a man who finds a wife finds what is good and receives favor from the Lord. Together, a man and a woman make a powerful union. There is a spirit enemy who understands that very power. One cannot avoid having difficulties in a marriage ordained by God. There are lots of relationships that give way to a next one that seems perfect. The problem with the second is that it may not be of God or, say, adulterous. The spirit enemy is fine with a man and a woman together in marriage if that union is against God's will. It is not what you have. The question is whether God is pleased with what you have. If you are in a marriage that is ungodly and cherish your soul, it is better to break up that marriage and be right with God. At the end, your spouse will put you in the grave alone to deal with God for the adulterous marriage that you were in. Better you stand for God's forgiveness in this life, than stand before Him for judgement after you die.

What Is Sexual Intercourse, or Sex?

101 Although it is treated as a commodity from a man's perspective, sex is not simply the most wonderful pleasure a woman provides to a man or a man to a woman. Yes, a man and a woman can simply jump into a sexual act to provide themselves with the pleasures humans' natural senses experience during sex. However, the true meaning and purpose of sex go beyond simple pleasures to the senses. God created sex for a man and a woman to be constantly and intimately in touch with each other.

Sex is not limited to sexual intercourse, but it can easily be reduced to just that. Sex is meant to happen between a man and a woman who are in a marital relationship or commitment. The marriage relationship guarantees that a man and woman will take care of each other as promised before they engaged in any sexual act.

Men and women differ in how they view sex. A man is constantly motivated by sex, and the woman will respond sexually when she feels loved, appreciated, and cherished. It does not require much effort for a woman to put any man in the mood for sex. However, for a woman to sexually desire a man, he needs to fit certain criteria, and there are some actions he must take. Certainly, this principle does not apply to all women, but it sure does to those women who desire a responsible man to build a proud family with in the society where they live.

Sex is a powerful tool for a woman. Like all power, sex can be misused by a female to control a relationship or any man who shows weakness in that area. Any normal man can fall weak before a woman he's attracted to. The only problem with some women using sex to control men or relationships is that those men are usually unfaithful to begin with. And the real values that keep a man with one woman faithfully has nothing to do with the woman but, rather, the man who understands a wife needs to be cared for and that there are enough issues and concerns having just one woman. The Christian values adopted by a wife help her marriage and will keep her from using her sexual power to control her husband. However, it is the man's responsibility to be the strong spiritual figure the woman needs. Most women have great respect for such men. A man who chases women just for sex loses all respect before them, especially before those women he used. And the woman who uses her sexual power to provoke men and to dominate over them is a curse to herself.

A Joyful Giver

102 No relationship is blessed where a spirit of fear is the prerequisite. Although wisdom comes as a result of fearing God—the Almighty, Creator of humankind—He does not intend to conceal His relationship with His children in fear of Him but in love. Much of the principles that serve as the foundation or ground in the relationship between Christ and the Church or God and His children are very similar to those that exist between husbands and wives. Although God or Jesus might be an authority over the church, it is not required that the church fear God or Jesus. The spirit of fear only pertains to the service that is obliged by those who serve, but love goes beyond. Healthy relationships know not fear but respect. Only in the absence of respect is

-102-

Perfect love bans all fear-Cf. 1 John 4:18

Those who follow Jesus for food and miracles-Cf. Matthew 4:4; John 6:27; Philippians 3:19

Giving up all for Jesus-Cf. Luke 12:33-34;

The presence of God is for those who love Him-Cf. Jeremiah 29:13; Matthew 5:8; Proverbs 8:17

Doing good without any expectations (Luke 6:35).

God loves a joyful giver (cf. 2 Corinthians 9:7).

that fear effective. But in the presence of love, it is not necessary to fear for love includes much respect.

Some glorify God in all circumstances. That is the presence of the love of God in their hearts. Others glorify God for the things He has done for them. The church is filled with those who are looking for God's favor and saying, "Thank you, Lord," for what He has done for them. However, true servants and people who want to walk with God are what is missing. It's the same in relationships between husbands and wives. Many husbands are in it for the sex, and wives are in the marriage for whatever husbands might be able to provide. None of them choose to be in service to each other. This is why there are so many fights and disagreements between married couples. The exchange always seems to be unfair. The woman feels that the man does not do enough for her to be generous to him. The man feels he does too much for her to ignore him and be indifferent toward him. Both become increasingly demanding of each other because they each place a very high price on their services and what they have to offer. This kind of relationship is based on nothing but the interests of the man, who is looking for sex, and the woman looking for security, protection, companionship, and all the rest. But none of them has considered that whatever attention they are looking for could more easily be found by being first in service to the other.

If you wish to receive anything from anyone, you must first sow a seed of the same thing you're looking for into that other person's life. If it is love you're looking for, you must first sow some love. You will receive much love in return. This is God's law of sowing and reaping. Whatsoever a man sows— or a woman, for that matter—he or she will also reap. There is absolutely no doubt about that. This works in the natural and in the divine. You cannot be stingy with what you have and have your eyes on what others have that you wish they would share with you. The secret is for you to give first, and it will then be given to you.

God so loved the world that He gave ... Someone who truly loves God will give up all possessions to seek the love of God in his or her heart. That doesn't mean that anyone can give anything in return for God's love. The giving of your possessions only proves your heart's desire and honesty about what you confessed from your mouth. Love is all about giving to another, and it does not have to be with any obligation or interest in mind.

The truth is that everyone will die whether one kept or gave everything he or she ever had. But one will only truly enjoy what was shared with someone else. The more of what you have that you legitimately share with others, the more of what you have you will truly enjoy. However, although God gives to all, even to those who are evil, He only shares His presence with those who show great need for Him. Those who are after God to obey Him are the only ones who gets to enjoy a true relationship with Him.

How does a man seek a woman without having sex in mind? And how does a woman seek a man without expecting him to make her feel loved? It is impossible for both the man and woman not to want

-103-

Women as weaker vessels (cf. 1 Peter 3:7).

The biblical definition of love (cf. 1 Corinthians 13:4–8; Colossians 3:14; Galatians 5:22; Proverbs 17:9).

anything from each other. Although we must seek to obey God, we must also expect from God. No expectations mean no worth, no value. We expect from God the same as God expects from us. The problem exists when expectations surpass the level and quality of giving. The more you want from something, the more you must put into it. However, for that there is limit. One must never invest time in something that will not produce good fruit. If you seek from someone who reluctantly gives or refuses to give, do not force yourself upon that individual. The joy is to receive from a joyful giver.

The Truth of the Word of God on the Matter of Sex

103 The relationship between a man and a woman is compared in the Bible with that of Christ Jesus and the church. In that passage, the apostle Paul defines this responsibility of a man toward his wife as a spiritual or complete provider. A true husband must give all his attention to his wife and watch over her, even in matters concerning her soul and salvation. Women, in another passage, are considered weak vessels, and their husbands must handle them with care and patience.

A woman needs a lot of attention. The greatest reward in that for the husband is not sex. That also is for the purpose of giving pleasure to the woman who feels loved and approved by her man. The greatest reward for a husband is the privilege of being a husband to his wife. It is a chance to be of service to her in that capacity. The happiest moment in the relationship between a married man and woman is when the man has not yet gotten her fully convinced to becoming his wife. That is the moment when he joyfully gives her the most attention, for he hasn't yet conquered what to him is a new territory. Once she became his wife, she needs to just submit in all things. And yes, this is what God requires her to do. But what about the husband's requirements to love his wife? How is this applied?

Based on the true definition of love, the husband has a more submissive requirement toward his wife than his wife toward him. The Bible describes love as being patient and unselfish; rather, one is to look in the interests of others. By that definition, one who's required to love must submit to the needs of others. God commands the wife to submit to her husband's authority and the husband to submit to the needs and cares of his wife at any time. A good husband is a slave to his wife's needs. While the world teaches men not to pay much attention to women, unless they need sex, God tells men to pay good attention to women and to love them. And men are programmed to think about women, not so they may sexually abuse them, but to care for them.

-104-

He who controls his emotion is greater than a great king (cf. *Proverbs 16:32; 25:28; 29:11; 15:18).*

Sexual Relations

104 Sex without the intimacy and personal rapport that must come beforehand is reserved for savages. There is no real satisfaction in simply acting in response to a need. A powerful and well-mannered human being is one who has great control over his or her emotions and can calculate reactions in response to needs. In vain, people try to control others without mastering control over themselves. No one can cause greater shame or create greater respect for anyone than oneself. And the individual can experience the great joy that comes from giving to others while controlling one's desires.

There is a universe of beings whose main disposition is to control their own desires and put themselves in service to others. They are those who practice the law of giving and receiving. They live to experience every day the joy of giving and avoid the disgust that results from selfishness and self-indulgence.

The greatest motivation is to be of service to those in need and a blessing to others. One who pursues the goodness of others will not have a place in his or her agenda to do evil and will stand before all as agent of the righteousness of God.

The principle of giving and receiving applied to sex will not only give a wife the greatest pleasure of knowing she is not being taken advantage of. In return, her husband will receive the pleasure of giving.

Spirit-Filled Advice about Your Sexual Partner

From a male perspective, sex is most enjoyable when giving pleasure. No man I have talked to has ever been satisfied being with a sexually nonresponsive female. Sex is an intimate moment shared between two individuals, male and female, to celebrate being together as one. It is best for both to be well pleased with each other before sharing that moment. One should not give the impression that he or she is doing the other a favor. And keep all sexual encounters in a well-secured marital relationship. It makes no sense to celebrate oneness with someone you are not really one with.

Topical biblical references: Choose your favorite Bible version to check the following references. The NIV is personally recommended.

-105-

It is the work of the flesh to provoke one another in our actions-Cf. Galatians 5:26

Domain 10

Service

To serve is to make yourself available to others. The hardest part in serving others is the important part; that is, to take their orders. The greatest servants among us are not those who have made the greatest sacrifices. Rather, they are those who have responded to the greatest needs of others.

Keeping a Serving Attitude

105 The world is all about being served. No one wants to be the one serving others. This portion addresses the benefits that exist in being a servant, as it is demanded of us in the Bible, and how important it is not to consider ourselves too highly before others.

People are boastful. Everyone needs to have the latest technology and wear the latest fashions. Let me very quickly say it is not wrong in itself to have the best for God Himself has given to all nothing but the best of all things. The problem in aspiring to have the best is in the motivation. If you seek stuff to provoke others, this is wrong. The parade of what you might not even own so others may see how much more blessed you are, or yet, how much better you are than those who do not have what you have, is bad motivation.

What Does the Bible Say about Blessings and Those Who Are Blessed?

106 To answer this question, one must first be able to differentiate true blessings from what appear to be blessings.

The answer is plain. Those who are blessed simply are so they may be blessings to others. A blessing, whatever it may be, is to help you better serve others. And where does that boastful spirit come from? If you said the devil, you have guessed very rightly.

One truth among humankind is that the only time God will favour you over someone else is when you use your potential better than another person. The living God is performance oriented. His only motivation is love, and His greatest turnoff is distrust. One who truly believes in God, follows His instructions, and is motivated by love for God and neighbors is a better person in the eyes of God. What is your motivation in life? What makes you get up early and go to bed late day after day? What dream are you trying to achieve, and how many will profit from that dream becoming a reality?

-106-

*Blessed to be a blessing-*Cf. *Matthew 5:16; Matthew 6:19-21*

*He who wishes to be great must serve others-*Cf. *Mark 9:35*

Judgment of all nations, in the last day- Cf. *Matthew 25:31-46*

The principal idea for living is to glorify God by how we act toward one another. We may do what is wrong toward each other and then use repentance and forgiveness to get back on track with others. Someone needs your abilities to make it through life, and God is the happiest when we are not constantly mad at one another or doing evil toward each other.

Everyone can do something that will benefit someone else. If any of the activities among humankind stops, many will suffer the consequences. We need bus drivers as much as doctors and teachers as much as housekeepers. All that is positive is necessary for the growth of our society.

So many of us have a burning desire in our hearts to do something, but we don't know what that is. Consequently, there is no peace in doing anything else. And once you intend to do what you must do, you will have no problem doing everything else. Chances are, you will not feel inferior doing what you consider small once you achieve your ultimate greatness.

The world needs your help, and mostly your dreams, to make it a better place for all humankind. You will not have peace until you do whatever good deeds you have in your heart to do. This is God's way of making sure everyone shares their dreams and makes great things happen to benefit us all. We are all blessed with something that can be useful to another person. Don't take your talents and experiences for granted. You will someday be held accountable for that which you did or did not do.

Live Free or Die

107 Life is a personal season of growth and shared moments and circumstances with others. You cannot ignore any aspect of life and still have a life. Many live and do not experience true living due to the lack of confidence in themselves that prevents them from sharing with others. Another group of people are very confident but do not trust others with the freedom to be themselves. No one's talent and intelligence is to interfere with another's ability to grow and the freedom of expression. People ought to be free to live, especially when they don't bother anyone else. A bird is a beautifully made creature. Although you may want to enjoy its existence, don't entertain the idea to cage it. Let others live.

What attitude must we have about those whose company we share? What must we expect from others to benefit us? Is it wrong to expect or demand goodness from others? How does one demand something from someone who does not have the disposition to give to others? How do we learn to suffer injustice? Must we always beg others for what they should normally give us? How do we define service? What do we freely give to others?

Our service to others is what identifies us to our world community. The more we can offer those around us, the more important we might become in that environment. The fact that many are looking to show themselves to the world through material possessions is only due to the fact that material possessions might represent the level of success we achieve from our

Those whose money is considered rotten and the cause of their own destructions. Cf. James 5:1-6; Proverbs 1:19

Stay away from those who love money- Cf. 1 Corinthians 5:11; Hebrews 13:5

The joy of sharing with others-Cf. Acts 20:35

No one should know when you give and share with others-Cf. Matthew 6: 3

To do unto others as you would want them to do onto you-Cf. Matthew 7: 12

Seek everyone interest, and not just your own-Cf. 1 Corinthians 10: 24 Philippians 2: 4

service to others. What we try to project is that we have much because we have contributed much, which is not always true. Nevertheless, many seek after status based on accumulating material possessions instead of focusing on the true riches that are based on real personal contributions to the world. Money is nothing if it does not represent an exchange of services rendered. It is important that we have money only to show that someone has received from us and as proof of a debt repaid. Your money should represent your great services rendered to others. Money cannot and should not stand on its own.

Human beings are selfish per nature when it comes to defending what they claim as their means of survival. They also demand much from others to assure their own well-being and comfort. Anything that requires a little inconvenience to benefit someone else is often refused.

Money is the greatest motivation for those who are selfish. And any favor or good deed to anyone is headline news. It is as if they made the greatest gesture to humanity, ignoring the fact that it is a natural duty for one to gladly do favors for others without the need to receive an award for it. The only and best reward for helping a fellow brother or sister is in the helping itself. One should be glad for the ability and opportunity to help someone, and the greatest pleasure is to keep it to yourself. Certainly, you must encourage one to serve others and maybe use yourself as an example. However, bragging about what you did for someone just for the sake of telling takes the honor out of your service.

Being self-centered has never guaranteed anyone the satisfaction that they look for, a satisfaction that is certainly guaranteed in focusing on the need of others. The joy we seek for ourselves is found in seeking that same joy for someone else.

People are selfish, and putting their own needs before those of others kills their chances to have their own needs fulfilled. Whatever need you have for yourself, look to honestly provide it to someone else. The joy you will find in gladly fulfilling the need of others will also serve you in the satisfaction of your own. There are Bible verses for this concept.

The Key to Life Is Service to Each Other

108 Life and the joy of it all is all about service to others. To be a great servant and able to enjoy it, you must rid yourself of all selfishness. A way to avoid being selfish is to have great control over personal desires. No desire will be fully controlled unless you are satisfied. You will never be truly satisfied without being truly submitted to God. If you are submitted to God, you must be willing to serve others. If you are confused by what you just read, read it again.

Flock Not with Unbelievers

109 You will not always get what you want from others, and that may sadden your soul very deeply. The truth is we cannot control how people act toward

-109-

Do not flock with unbelievers (cf. 2 Corinthians 6:14; James 4:4; Hebrews 3:12; Ephesians 5:11; 1 Corinthians 10:21; Ephesians 5:6–11).

To be the light of the world (cf. Matthew 5:14–16).

Be truthful to one another (cf. Proverbs 12:22; Ephesians 4:25; Colossians 3:9)

Your reasonable service to God (cf. Romans 12:1-21)

us, even when we try to act toward them with the greatest consideration. People will betray the kindest person if they happen to disagree about an important aspect of life; like faith, for example. The saying, "Birds of a feather flock together," is true. Those who agree on things will go easier together. And those who respect the boundaries set by others experience better love and appreciation from many. If you wish to be loved by the world, you must accept the world as is. Therefore, if your desires—like mine—tend to lean toward what is right, you may not experience the love and consideration of many. However, there is a peace reserved for those whose faith and desires disagree with the norm. There is a tranquility of the mind and soul available for all who seek order in the world. No one is called to change the world, not even those with the greatest talents, abilities, and knowledge. Not even those who seem to have the potential to do so. As it is written: "Be not overcome of evil, but overcome evil with good." Romans 12:21 King James Version

Although it is difficult to consider, we are all called to good deeds toward each other, no matter how different we are in our faiths and opinions. People will receive from us what we offer to them if we present ourselves as true as possible. One will never be able to sell anyone something in which he or she doesn't believe in or isn't driven by. People look to be inspired more than to be convinced. So instead of pressing ourselves on others and wishing your desires upon them, invite them to go on a journey with you. You do win people by showing off, but you will also lose a lot more when they discover that the truth is not in you. One cannot preach life and show misery, and you cannot speak of love and show indifference or hate.

Peace is not found in being in perfect agreement with others. Rather, it is found in being in agreement with ourselves about what we believe and the true life we live before others. Peace is found in true service to others. Those who argue with the core of your being, your dreams, and your beliefs are not to flock with.

Spirit-Filled Advice about Serving Others

It is very important that we first cultivate whatever talent and abilities we are born with before presenting ourselves to others. The level of our service to others must be in the exact proportion with our education and training. We are not to limit ourselves simply to attending school or successfully completing a program at a prestigious institution. To be knowledgeable means that we need to be open-minded. Wisdom and knowledge are of unlimited measure, and they are found in unlikely places. Many great inventions were bumped into by people who looked for creations and knowledge beyond the walls of renowned universities. Education of all kinds needs to be valued. The greatest level of knowledge requires a great deal of self-involvement, not just attending the greatest schools.

Topical biblical references: Choose your favorite Bible version to check the following references. The NIV is personally recommended.

Consideration to the needs of others *(cf. Philippians 2:4).*

-110-

Be productive and achieve all that you find good to do *(cf. Titus 3:14; Ephesians 4:28; Galatians 6:9; Proverbs 18:9; Luke 3:11; Romans 12:11–13; 1 Timothy 6:18; Colossians 3: 23–25; Ephesians 6: 7–8; Proverbs 22:29; 6:6–8; 21:5; 10:4; Psalms 37:4; Proverbs 14:23; Proverbs 13:4; Proverbs 12:2–4).*

Domain 11
Indifference

Indifference is to have and to show no interest or concern for what is going on around us. Indifferent is to say, "It's not my job." It is also passing on your moment and opportunity to shine before God while helping someone. To be indifferent is the exact opposite of to love. You cannot be a Christian and be indifferent to the needs of others when you can help.

Destiny—Only You Can Do This

110 People need people; that is an undeniable truth. Whether a person honors your presence in his or her life, that person needs your existence to continue to exist. You as a person may not be important to anyone, but the role you play in others' lives, along with your personality, is one of a kind. Many will fall into your category and have your level of competence, but no one will ever be able to play your role in a person's life. That is yours to fill. No one will be able to fulfill your destiny regarding others. It is your job to do what only you have the chance to do. And if you choose not to, someone will play your role, but no one will accomplish your God-given mission for you.

One of the greatest misconceptions in life is that someone will replace you and do what you were supposed to do as a husband, parent, friend, or even someone's simple acquaintance. It is possible that your spouse will marry another person after you have departed, and that someone will mother or father your children in your place. The person who will then be in your place, playing your role, will never be you. Nor will the individual ever be able to undo the goodness and experiences you gave those who shared your existence. You will be as memorable as you are faithful to your destiny regarding those around you. Whether they are friends, family, or complete strangers, you owe everyone you meet during life the provision that God has placed in you for them. No one can do it for you.

Many fail to fulfill their destinies based on the excuse that their lives and purposes in others' lives are not as important as those of other people who are considered great by society's standard. Some feel they have missed their chances or are not educated enough. Others let themselves be discouraged by circumstances or fall into the temptation of seeking empty treasures that will never satisfy. Treasures like a great job, a successful career, or even a great marriage with the spouse of your dreams and having children will never make up for not doing what God has called you to do. Nothing else satisfies than being in the middle of God's will. The world is filled with miserable success.

The Many Types of Service and Disservice

111 God leaves no rooms for people to be neutral in the service they need to render to others. One can either be of service or disservice to your fellow neighbors. The greatest motivation to humankind ought to be service. Everyone needs to render a service to others to be considered a functioning part of society. It is true that most people like to be served, and no one likes to be inconvenienced by serving someone else. However, the greatest reward is in the service we give, not in what we receive.

You cannot be indifferent regarding others and the service you are ordained by God to provide to them. Don't keep yourself from offering your best to others, not just for your benefit, but also for the benefit of those to whom you offer your service. To be indifferent is a sin against God, yourself, and those who suffer your indifference. It is the exact opposite of love.

There is plenty to do. If you cannot start something on your own, be part of someone else's business or movement. However possible, keep moving. Get involved in something that benefits others. God blesses those who are in the business of being a blessing to others.

-111-

Your call from God to service and good works (cf. Hebrews 10:24; 1 Peter; 4:10; Galatians 6:10).

He Who knows good and does not do it has committed a sin (cf. James 4:17).

If you see your neighbor in need and close your eyes, you sin against God (cf. 1 John 3:18–19).

Spirit-Filled Advice about Indifference

It may be personal, but I have found that the greatest form of indifference is embedded in those who refuse to learn. Many aspire to achieve great goals without having to invest the necessary time to be able to serve in that capacity. It is a great disservice to others to be mediocre at anything. Even if it is washing dishes, one should be disposed to being the best he or she can be. One should not want to rely 100 percent on others to achieve a personal dream. Invest in the talent of others, but cultivate your own talent and be a real inspiration to others while reaching for the person you need to become.

Domain 12

Love

To love is to truly play a great role in the lives of others. Love is the faithful practice of the justice of God. To love is the one new commandment given by Jesus to His disciples. It is the fulfillment of the law.

> "Master, which is the great commandment in the law?
> Jesus said unto him, Thou shalt love the Lord thy God with all thy heart, and with all thy soul, and with all thy mind.
> This is the first and great commandment.
> And the second is like unto it, Thou shalt love thy neighbour as thyself.
> On these two commandments hang all the law and the prophets."
> Matthew 22:36-40 King James Version

Love Rejected

112 To truly understand the impact of love in any relationship and grasp its meaning, one must consider the love of God for humanity and the consequences of such a love being rejected by humankind. The Bible says that God so loves the world. That love of God was proven by Him in such a way that no one who believes can deny that it is, in fact, a great sacrifice made in the name of love.

But what if someone says, "I don't believe that it is true." In fact, many don't believe in God's love for humankind. The question that usually comes with their unbelief is this. If God so loves the world, why does He allow so much suffering? The answer to that question is simple. The world today is the consequence of the world's rejection of the love of God.

Love is nothing but a predisposition to performing good actions. What if someone you love refuses to accept any favors from you? What will become of your predisposition to doing good deeds towards that person. The answer is nothing. Your love is your love, and all your predispositions and favors toward anyone who doesn't accept your love will only be made available for that person, but it will never be profitable to that individual. It is the same for the love of God for humanity and maybe your love for a child or spouse. You may love your family to death, but if they are unwilling to submit under your loving care, all your efforts to help them are futile. You cannot force your love on anyone, and neither will God.

What is the greatest commandment? (cf. *Matthew 22:38*).

To be rejected by your own people (cf. *John 1:11*).

What does it mean to love God? (cf. *Psalm 97:10; Proverbs 13:5*).

God's love and sacrifice for those who yet do not love Him (cf. *Romans 5:8*).

The conditional love of God (cf. *John 14:21; Hosea 9:15; Psalm 5:5; Leviticus 20:23; Proverbs 6:16–19; Acts 10:35; Ephesians 5:5–6*).

Why Would Such a Great Love Like that of God Be Rejected?

113

He who does not love God loves death (cf. Proverbs 8:36).

God loves all without exceptions Luke 6:35

113 Love demands a great deal of understanding. It also comes with the greatest price tag, which is your freedom. Everyone understands that it means nothing to accept a little favor from those who may show interest in them. However, when it comes to accepting someone's love, you might want to ask, what is expected in return for that love? And this is where most people might become really concerned whether they should accept love from another person.

This love is an agreement between two people to submit to one another, like the love shared in a marriage relationship. Not many are comfortable with the agreement to submit to another person. Instead, everyone is looking for someone to submit to them.

If you have your own way of doing things and then suddenly come face-to-face with a desire to have a someone in your life, there's a lot to consider. Both you and that person will experience many changes if the two of you agree to consummate that desire. You will have to submit to that person as you expect that person to submit to you. What is it to submit is an entirely different situation.

The love Jesus shared with His disciples, for example, is presented in an agreement. Jesus declared, "If you love me, keep my commandments." This is not in any way a light requirement. But this kind of love requires a commitment from both parties involved to fulfill all the blessings accompanying this type of love. This love is relational, so it requires a relationship to develop in.

There is a love that is unconditional. It is the love of God for humanity. There is another type of love that one must submit to its conditions for it to be effective, like the love of doctors for their patients. The doctor cannot tell the patient, "Go ahead, and do whatever you want with your health. I got your back." Your doctor may have your back, but if you abuse your health, you'll certainly pay the consequences, and there is nothing your loving doctor can do to avoid those consequences that result from your bad choices with your health.

It is the same for those you come to love. They will tell you that if really you love them, you must accept them with all their nonsense. You may love them, of course, but what good is your love if you stand and watch them ruin their lives while all you can say is, "I love you." What kind of nonsense would that be? Your good knowledge should benefit those you love. If you can't come into a loving agreement with those you love, your love is no use to them. You must be able to share concerns with those you love.

Many have raised a barrier between them and God's love for them. They place their own conditions on being loved by God. Their conditions limit how deep God can get involved in their personal lives. Their intentions are for God to bless them, but they don't necessarily have to obey His rules for Him to bless and protect them.

What about your conditions for accepting someone's love? What must someone do to prove to

-114-

To love difficult people- (cf. Matthew 5:43-48; Luke 6:27-36)

Showing your love toward God by loving your neighbor (cf. 1 John 4:20).

Love is the fulfillment of all the laws given to Moses and the prophets (cf. Romans 13:8, 10; Matthew 22:40; Galatians 5:14).

you that he or she loves you? What kind of ransom do you place on permission to love you? What is your requirement to be loved?

A lot has been said about love, and great sacrifices have been offered in the name of love. However, although what has been said and the sacrifices are well received, love itself will not be honored easily for people are not willing to submit themselves to anyone. You sacrifice yourself in vain to prove your love to someone if he or she refuses to consider your advice. People want to be loved but do not want to enter into any agreement where someone tells them or advises them about their faults or wrongdoings.

Free Love to All

114 The Bible requires that we love everyone. You are free to love your enemies as it is required for you to do. This is the kind of love that God also has for humanity. Although people may not accept Him, He shows favors toward them anyway.

Such a love is freely given. It does not require anything from anyone to receive it. It is the blessing of God upon all. But this love is like free medicine without any instructions and no consultation. Although it may be a great gift, without the related instructions, that gift might become dreadful.

One needs to enter into agreement with God to fully benefit from His love and kindness. You also need to enter into agreement with one another to benefit from the love that we share.

The greatest type of love is that which we all crave. It is manifest in the closest human relationship, which is known as intimacy. Love remains love, but it is in the closeness of humanity that the simplest love is brewed to greatness. We know God best in our intimate relationship with the Almighty through prayer. We also become one with our spouses through intimacy. You cannot share a meaningful love with any being by keeping your distance from that being.

The free and unconditional love we share with each other is insufficient to transform us into the perfect creations we were created to be. We need not only use the free gifts and blessings of God. We must also come into a great relationship with God, where the love He has for us will blossom to its fullness. That love also needs to be cultivated in a great relationship with each other to truly experience life as it is meant to be.

The Effectiveness of Love

115 The Bible tells us that love covers a multitude of sins. The practice of love toward one another is the secret to living together as a community. It's not for no reason that Jesus gave this new commandment: Love is the fulfillment of all the laws. One who loves God and his or her neighbors fulfills the entire Ten Commandments. We have heard that no one is able to observe the entire law of God. But Jesus now tells us this commandment fulfills it all. The entire creation has been made perfect through the practice of love. That makes love the only thing that matters

-115-

Love helps balance the difference among the many characters of society, and covers their multitude of sins (cf. 1 Peter 4:8; Proverbs 10:12; Proverbs 17:9; James 5:20; 1 Peter 1:22).

to us all. It is the only precept that is proven effective and successful in human relationships.

Love, as you must know, is not the feeling you have when you meet a person who fits perfectly on your list of the most desirable people. Rather, it is the effort you must make to get along with that person qualified as number one on your crap list. Love is described in the Bible as both what is and what is not love. It is necessary so no one makes the mistake of confusing love with some type of emotion. Love is not what you felt for your spouse-to-be at the beginning of your relationship. It is the techniques you applied after you found out this person is nothing like you. Love is the exercise that can transform your desires into tolerance for anyone, so you can discover the beauty that truly exists in that person. It is okay that you are lied to by your own expectations of others. But you need to realize there are far more beauties beyond what you perceived in your mind, and you don't have to share all aspects of every single person. What you call different in them belongs to someone else for them share with. You cannot limit someone to please just you. What about God in that person's life? I am positive that you and God have different expectations from that person you hold dear. Love will help you cultivate the ability to accept what you will from a person and leave the rest for whom it belongs. The Creator God had you in mind when He was creating your best friend or spouse. However, you weren't the only person He had in mind. Society is formed of a variety of individuals with different characters. Love is the only formula that guarantees the getting along of all those characters and the success of any society.

Spirit-Filled Advice about Love Issues

It is not easy to accept in others what you have spent your life trying to reject. Often what you detest in others is a trait that is deeply embedded in you. Learn to forgive others as you would wish to be forgiven by them. Do not keep offences from others. Release those who have somehow offended you. Forgiveness is just like a reset button that enables us to continue achieving a goal we set before we discovered the imperfections in all of us.

Conclusion

A Sick World

116 The world is sick in its spirit. The only medicines that will cure it are repentance and forgiveness. People wake up every day doing what is detrimental to their physical, mental, and spiritual health. Many are living with symptoms that they purposely ignore. Others die every day because of their disobedience and stubbornness. Still, people are not so prompt to repent. Not many like to admit they are wrong and going in the wrong direction. So you find many who are continuing in their sins, causing themselves what they would only wish on their worst enemies.

Sin knows no favoritism. It will kill you and your enemies. It will also kill those who acknowledge it, and those who don't. And whether your sin is fun or painful, dying from it will always be regretful. There will always be something that you wish you had done when you are close to being dead. The most common time of repentance for many is death. However, many will not have the chance to see that coming. Yes, many of us will not have that last chance to repent.

Topical biblical references- Chose your favorite bible version to check the following references. The NIV is personally recommended.

-116-

The act of repentance- (cf. Acts 3:19)

The wages of sin are death- (cf. Romans 6:23)

No one knows the days and how their death will come- (cf. Ecclesiastes 9:12)

Do not harden your heart or sadden the spirit- (cf. Hebrews 3:8)

Don't kill your conscience- (cf. Thessalonians 5:19-22; Romans 13:5)

-117-

The company of evil is to be avoided- (cf. 1 Corinthians 15: 33 Psalm 1:1-4)

Walk with the wise- (cf. Proverbs 13:20)

What is the price of your soul? - (cf. Matthews 16: 26 Mark 8:36-37)

Judgment of all nations, in the last day- (cf. Matthew 25: 31-46)

Our spiritual sickness is the best opportunity that we must repent and turn from our wrong ways of living. All sickness in the spirit has a sign or symptom that will tell you something is wrong. If you feel uneasy about an old and lasting bad habit, or you feel ashamed or uncomfortable every time you go some places with some friends, stop and think about it. Consider talking with someone with better moral or spiritual values. Don't ignore your feelings about things you think are going wrong in your life. Deal with your spirit; don't kill it. Death may come without warning, so at least be right with yourself in the days of your life.

The Point of It All

117 Everyone wakes up every day to the same two opportunities: to do good or to do evil to those we meet. If you have control over how to act and react toward those around you, you have control over life itself. Every good or bad moment that we experience can be made better or worse by those whose company we are in. No one can prevent anyone from experiencing problems in life, but the company of great people will ease your troubles.

Life is not as complicated as it feels. The challenges we face every day are caused by people who are either being indifferent or violent to us. And every wise person knows that the greatest cause of violence among humankind is selfishness. People live to prosper at the expense of others and without gratitude, because if they should be grateful, then they would be obliged to reward others for helping them achieve their prosperity. Gratitude demands that you have consideration for others, and for most people, that's too high a cost to pay just to be kind.

We are an extremely busy generation going nowhere. Our businesses, which focus on making life easier and more convenient, take precious time away from the real business that we are here to take care of. Our determination to achieve success has taken away the most precious aspects of life and left us with a purposeful but meaningless life. What will it serve someone to have much in possession at the cost of one's soul? What will it profit you to accomplish your dream if it brings you no peace. It is the same as selling your family to slavery to have food in the house and then have no one to eat with. It is good to dream big dreams; it is better to dream with others and have them with you on your journey. We must make time for people because they are the point of it all.

The Business of Soul

118 What does it profit someone to gain the whole world and loose his or her soul? The only real possession of any being on earth is one's soul. There is no other thing that is more precious to an individual than the soul. Your soul will always be part of you. It will not part from you when you die. Your soul is the only thing you will take with you into the afterlife. Got it? The saying, "He who dies with the most toys wins," would make sense only if he who died could take with him all the toys that he accumulated. If we

-118-

To prosper as your soul prospers- (cf. 3 John 1:2)

The fruit of the flesh- (cf. Galatians 5:19-21)

Having no respect for the blood of Jesus- (cf. Hebrews 10:29)

The first coming of Jesus to save the world- (cf. John 3:17)

The chance to be reconciled with God- (cf. 2 Corinthians 5: 18-19)

The happiness in heaven- (cf. Luke 15:7)

One death, then comes the judgement of God- (cf. Hebrews 9:27)

For it is written, that everyone will come face to face with Jesus- (cf. 1 Corinthians 13:12)

For it is written, that everyone will come face to face with Jesus- (cf. 1 Corinthians 13:12)

251

never understand anything in life, this we must make sure we all get. Nothing has any real importance unless it affects our soul, and we know no real joy unless we are at peace in our souls. All other things that we might experience are simply moments of satisfaction that may cause even more pain to our souls. The ancient word of wisdom says to guard your heart—in other words, your soul—above all things. So what do you need to do to guarantee that your soul is safe?

Your soul is the set of emotions that enables humankind to feel pain or joy. Your soul is what will cause you to feel pain in hell if you get yourself there. Your soul cannot make it to heaven if you have all kinds of filth in it; for instance, hatred, jealousy, and hypocrisy. It is your responsibility to make sure your soul is saved, meaning that it is heavenly trained before you die.

The greatest thing is that Jesus died to pay the price for all our mistakes, otherwise known as sin. However, deliberately doing what is wrong and making a habit of it. Or worse, never go before God in Jesus's name to ask forgiveness for your sins, in prayer. For that, we have no excuse. As the Bible says, this is like stomping your feet on the blood of Jesus.

God cares enough to have gone through all the pain of sending Jesus to die, so you may save your soul. As this wasn't enough, He provides you with all kind of messengers. People lose sleep to create ways and write books to warn you about your soul. All you need to do is to accept Jesus's sacrifice to have died on the cross for your sins. Ask God to forgive you of your sins. Follow Jesus's teachings on how to rid your soul of the filth of the pass and fill your heart with the love of God.

Adam sinned and put us in the condition we are in. Because of him, we are vulnerable to sin and have developed all kinds of bad habits. But it is not his fault that we remain in that condition. We do not have to live angry with ourselves and others. We can reconcile with God and be at peace with ourselves and others. Simply to avoid the experience of living in hell here on earth and then hell in the afterlife is enough reason for anyone to accept Jesus. Accepting Jesus does not change anything about Jesus. Certainly, heaven is happy every time a lost soul is turned back to God. Accepting Jesus, however, benefits the person who accepts Him. Accepting that Jesus has paid the price for your sinful nature reconciles you with God. By doing so, you're back on track with your true destiny.

Living according to your sinful nature puts you on the same plan and with the same destiny as the devil. Satan's destiny is eternal destruction in hell. Those who accept Jesus have changed from complete destruction to the complete peace of God.

Your soul needs to be reconnected with God, so you may learn how to live, not according to bad habits and personal emotions, but by the Spirit and according to wisdom. According to the Word of God.

Printed in the United States
By Bookmasters